D1559611

HART CRANE AND YVOR WINTERS

HART CRANE AND YVOR WINTERS

Their Literary Correspondence

THOMAS *Francis* PARKINSON

UNIVERSITY OF CALIFORNIA PRESS

Berkeley   Los Angeles   London

PS
3505
R272
Z547

University of California Press
Berkeley and Los Angeles, California

University of California Press, Ltd.
London, England

ISBN: 0-520-03538-0
Library of Congress Catalog Card Number: 77-80475
Copyright © 1978 by The Regents of the University of California

1 2 3 4 5 6 7 8 9 0

Printed in the United States of America

For James D. Hart and

Janet Lewis Winters

CONTENTS

PREFACE AND ACKNOWLEDGMENTS

The dedication of this book to James D. Hart and Janet Lewis Winters gives some sense of my gratitude for their substantial aid and my admiration of their persons. Professor Hart, when I was an undergraduate student, introduced me to the systematic study of modern criticism and poetry and has been a steady friend and helpful colleague for many years. As Director of the Bancroft Library of the University of California at Berkeley, he saw the merit of the Crane-Winters papers and gathered the funds necessary for their purchase. Mrs. Winters spent long hours discussing her memories of Arthur Yvor Winters and filling in gaps in his biography. She was unfailingly generous and hospitable and illuminating, bringing to our conversations the incisive intelligence, the clear imagination, and the profound sense of literature that have made her one of the most distinguished writers of the century. I prize my memories of those hours, and I prize above all the friendship that has grown from them.

Allen Tate was a patient and generous correspondent, and he called my attention to the presence of Winters's letters to him in the Princeton Library. The Princeton Library was cooperative in every way, as were the Beinecke Library at Yale University, the Harriet Monroe Poetry Library at the University of Chicago, the Butler Library of Columbia University, the Alderman Library at the University of Virginia, the library of the Rosenbach Foundation Museum, and above all the Bancroft Library at the Univer-

sity of California at Berkeley. Estelle Rebec was a model of coop-
eration, as were other members of the staff of the Bancroft
Library.

Brom Weber, who holds the rights to Hart Crane's letters was,
as always, friendly and helpful, and the Crane letters are reproduced with his permission. Janet Lewis Winters, after consulta-
tion with her lawyer, permitted me to cite facts and judgments
from Winters's letters to Harriet Monroe and Allen Tate. According to the terms of Winters's will, none of his letters can be quoted
directly until 1993, twenty-five years after his death. Allen Tate
permitted the reproduction of one of his three extant letters to
Yvor Winters. There is in the scholarly world some confusion
about the right to print letters. Mere physical ownership of a letter does not entail the right to reproduce any portion of the letter
without the permission of the writer or literary executor or the
holder of the rights to the letters. I have been extremely careful in
following this law. Unfortunately, graduate school training in
English is not all that it could be, so that even holders of the doctorate are frequently unaware of this fundamental legal principle. Violations of it can have very serious consequences.

Of the letters reproduced in this book, all but one of the letters
from Crane to Winters are in the Bancroft Library, and they
have been used with the permission of the library and of Brom
Weber. One letter—that of November 1, 1926—is in the library
of the University of Virginia and is used with the permission of
that library and of Professor Weber. The letter from Allen Tate
to Winters is in the hands of Janet Lewis Winters and is used with
her permission and that of Tate. In reproducing the letters I have
silently corrected minor misspellings; it might be interesting to
know that Crane invariably spelled immediately *immeadiately,*
but there seems no reason to clutter the pages with *sic.* Crane normally spelled very well, and he wrote wonderful letters, clear,
energetic, amusing, and often profound. In the near future there
should certainly be an edition of his complete letters, and that
will be the place for reproduction of his minor typos and gaffes,
not such a book as this.

One pleasure of teaching at Berkeley is the friendliness of stu-

dents and colleagues. The text has been read and improved by
Professors Jonas Barish, Josephine Miles, and Alex Zwerdling. I
could not always accept their suggestions, but they saved me from
occasional awkwardness in the writing and some doubtful interpretations. Many of the merits of the book are theirs; all the
faults are mine. Two fine graduate students, Penelope Nesbitt
and Cornelia Nixon, helped prepare the typescript and made
important suggestions. Nesbitt prepared the final copy and
checked the notes and bibliography with her usual scrupulous
care. The students in English 208 put up with my obsession with
Crane and Winters for several weeks and were tolerant and
amused and very helpful in their candor and good sense.

Drs. Lovell Langstroth and Anthony Engelbrecht saw me
through a dangerous illness while the book was being finished,
and without their friendliness and encouragement, the book
would have been delayed and perhaps never finished.

Chapters one and two were printed in a different form in
Southern Review, and it is a pleasure to tender acknowledgment
to the magazine and to Donald E. Stanford. Part of chapter six
and of the Introduction were printed in an earlier form in *Ohio
Review,* and special thanks are due to the magazine and to
Wayne Dodd and Calvin Thayer.

The photograph of Hart Crane is pasted into Winters's copy of
White Buildings and is reproduced with the permission of the
Bancroft Library. The photograph of Yvor Winters is repro-
duced with the permission of Janet Lewis Winters.

The information in the appendix was made accessible through
the courtesy of the Stanford Archives in the Stanford Library and
was augmented by conversations with Janet Lewis Winters and
Professor Virgil Whitaker.

Peter Howard of Serendipity Books gave freely of his time and
knowledge and friendship. He first called my attention to the existence of the letters from Crane to Winters. The purchase of the
Crane-Winters material was made possible by the Chancellor's
Opportunity Fund and The Friends of the Bancroft Library. The
Committee for Research at the University of California at Berkeley was, as it steadily has been, a source of monetary support.

My wife Ariel has asked to be left out of the acknowledgments, believing that such mention is a conventional gesture that she does not need or deserve. She is quite wrong, since her presence and that of our daughter Chrysa made all the difference.

Finally, I return to James D. Hart and Janet Lewis Winters, one a great scholar and teacher, the other a great novelist and poet. I hope the book is worthy of them.

T. P.

Berkeley, 1974-1977

INTRODUCTION

It is tempting to think of Crane and Winters as antithetical figures: the critical professor and the bohemian poet; the family
man living a stable life in a favored rural and academic atmosphere, and the reluctant homosexual (Allen Tate's characteriza-
tion of Crane) whose drinking and insuperable problems with his
parents destroyed his genius; the prominent and even notorious
figure in the literary circles of New York and Paris, and the
remote scholar in the solitude of Palo Alto. This schematic sense
has tended to dominate one of the most interesting and sympto-
matic literary relationships of the twentieth century. For years it
has been miscomprehended, and it will probably never be completely understood.

The evidence has until recently been very limited. From biog-
raphies of Crane it has been known that Winters encouraged his
work in correspondence, but exactly what Winters wrote has not
been known and probably never will be. Crane appreciated Winter's' letters, as he wrote to Mrs. T. W. Simpson ("Aunt Sally"),
his friend and companion during his stay at the Isle of Pines,
where he wrote most of *The Bridge* and underwent the direct experience of a hurricane that destroyed his family's house in which
he was staying.

Winters continues to write me most stimulating criticism;
his wide scholarship not only in English literature but in

xiv INTRODUCTION

Latin, Greek, French and Spanish and Portuguese—gives his statements a gratifying weight.[1]

Vindicating his work to his mother, he quoted from a letter by Winters responding to the publication of *White Buildings:*

> Yvor Winters, who is a professor of French and Spanish at the Moscow University, Idaho, writes me the following: "Your book arrived this evening, and I have read it through a couple of times. It will need many more readings, but so far I am simply dumbfounded. Most of it is new to me, and what I had seen is clarified by its setting. I withdraw all minor objections I have ever made to your work—I have never read anything greater and have read very little as great."[2]

A month later he was complaining to Allen Tate that he could not keep up with the cascade of letters from Winters in isolation at Moscow:

> I wish I could keep up with Winters. I already owe him several letters, besides comment on the ms. of his "Fire Sequence," which awaited me when I returned from town. All his work is so genuine that it takes close attention, meditation and blood and bone to answer.[3]

The relation was not that of Winters the critic to Crane the poet but of two young students and writers of poetry who took serious interest in each other's work. From Winters's critical writing it is clear that he admired Crane's work, although his opinions underwent substantial change, from his enthusiastic reception of *White Buildings* in 1927 to his predominantly negative review of *The Bridge* in 1930 to his essay on "The Significance of *The Bridge* by Hart Crane or What Are We to Think of Professor X?" in 1947 and his later and dimmer views of the merits of Crane's work.[4] By 1967 he saw no value in Crane's poetry. But for several of his most important years, Crane's writing was at the center of his thought.

Winters was a demon letter writer. Between January 30 and February 1 of 1927 he wrote four separate letters to Allen Tate, and that indicates why Crane grumbled about the problem of keeping up with Winters. His habit of extensive correspondence developed from his isolation from literary centers. As Winters wryly noted in the introduction to his *Early Poems,* "In the 'twenties I was not in Paris, nor even at Harvard."[5] Practically all of Winters's life was spent in the western United States. Only late in life did he venture east of Chicago, and his stays then were brief, if one excludes a summer at the Kenyon School of Criticism. Once he and Janet Lewis Winters went to the airport for a flight to New York, only to discover that the planes were grounded because of snow at the New York airport. He canceled the trip.[6]

Hence the writing of letters was one way to compensate for literary conversation beyond that provided by students and colleagues at Stanford. His correspondence was immense and generous. When Hart Crane lost his possessions in the hurricane at the Isle of Pines, he offered him financial aid, and when Allen Tate was in financial straits he offered to help him. In both instances, he had not met either man, but he loved their work. As Janet Lewis said, when this subject and other acts of generosity by Winters came up, "We were all poor together." In that great productive era from 1912 through the 1930s, men of letters seem to have felt a sense of mutual responsibility — after all, nobody else cared or was expected to care. They were, most of them, poor, but not in spirit.

The correspondence with Crane and Tate was only part of Winters's way of maintaining his connections and extending them. He wrote to Harriet Monroe and to Marianne Moore in their roles as editors. Glenway Wescott once wrote to Winters in a panic because he had mislaid copies of his poems; Winters sent him the copies he had in his hands. Some of Winters's letters to the editors of *Hound and Horn* were printed without his permission, and to his annoyance, but the discourtesy and illegality he allowed to pass, in spite of Allen Tate's request that he join him in a legal suit; at the time, Winters was dying. He wrote to numerous people, and as his fame increased younger writers sent letters and poems to him, so that Donald Davie, for example, carried on a sizable correspondence with Winters.

The bulk of letters passing from Stanford to New York and Chicago and England and back must have been a massive quarry for scholarship in poetry written in English from 1918 to 1968. A fair number of letters from Winters have survived, though by the terms of his will they cannot be published until 1993. Of the letters sent to Winters, practically all have been destroyed.

There remain some few miscellaneous letters of real interest, and one collection that clarifies the relations between Winters and Crane and provides basic information about the poetics of both men. The other letters from Winters's friends and colleagues in the literary world were destroyed over the years as they outlived their utility and importance to him. At the close of his life he became more systematic. He and Janet Lewis together burned their letters to each other. When I asked how she felt at that moment, she said mildly, "I felt sad."

I imagine that Winters also felt sad, and many recipients of letters from W. H. Auden were saddened and bewildered by his will that asked that all personal letters from him be destroyed. In his will Winters interdicted the publication of any letters from him until twenty-five years after his death, and he made the ultimate interdiction by destroying practically all letters to him.

He did not destroy the letters from Hart Crane. Between October 25, 1926, and December 10, 1928, Crane wrote at least forty-two letters and two postcards to Winters, a little more than half of them concerned with his own poetry, especially *The Bridge*. He included with the letters segments of *The Bridge* and other poems, so that Winters had read and commented on all but three sections of the poem by the end of 1928. The remainder of Crane's letters contain extremely sensitive and appreciative criticism of the early poems of Winters.

After December 10, 1928, the correspondence breaks off until Crane resumes it with apologies on January 14, 1930, with a letter that included a carbon copy of the final text of *The Bridge*. A final letter of January 27 thanks Winters for his willingness to review *The Bridge* and describes the editions from The Black Sun

Press and Boni and Liveright. After Winters's review appeared, Crane wrote him a furious letter that Winters did not care to keep. For all practical purposes, the correspondence stops with the letter of January 27, 1930.

Of these letters, only one has been printed in Brom Weber's edition of the *Letters of Hart Crane*. Half of the letters are five hundred or more words in length; very few of them are in any sense perfunctory. They have biographical interest, but they are primarily important as expressions of Crane's mature sense of poetics. They are written in a tone of affectionate and sometimes playful respect.

These letters were not preserved accidentally. They were carefully contained in two folders. Speculating on Winters's reasons for saving these letters, I wrote to Allen Tate and asked his views, since he was Winters's chief correspondent other than Crane during the period from late 1926 to 1930. He suggested that Winters may have kept the letters as documentary evidence against the charge that he had deliberately attempted to destroy Crane's poetic reputation, that preserving the letters was a justified act of self-vindication.

They do in part serve that purpose, but my own view is that the preservation of these letters is best illuminated by the destruction of Winters's and Janet Lewis's letters to each other. Winters like Matthew Arnold and T. S. Eliot had a sense of rectitude and reticence, the belief that his public views were spread before the world, that he had made of those views what he could and the world could make of them what the world would. Neither Arnold nor Eliot wanted an authorized biography, and by the terms of his will Winters deferred the possibility of any full biography until 1993 and made a biographer's task practically impossible by destroying the papers in his possession.

Following this logic, I should say that Winters felt that the Crane letters were of more than private interest and that they would hold a central place in public and historical judgment of Crane's character and his poetry. Beyond that, they show Crane at his most engaging and charming. Filtered by three thousand miles, Crane appears without his famous rages, his destructiveness to furniture, himself, and others, his drunkenness, the details of his experience which attract and repel biographers and commentators. There is a purity to them, an overriding sense of devotion to the art and life of poetry. We should be grateful that geography in the 1920s was real in a way that, in this age of easy impulsive flight from coast to coast and continent to continent, it is not.

In this correspondence, Crane was also relieved from considering his financial troubles and his difficulties with his family. He and Winters were to meet only once, under happy circumstances in southern California during Christmas week of 1927. Throughout their correspondence, even after that meeting, they addressed each other as Winters and Crane, not an uncommon habit at the time but indicating the professional nature of their friendly and intimate relationship. The professional utility of the correspondence helped Crane on a practical level and lifted him from the bog of his personal problems.

Winters used the letters when he wrote his lengthy essay on Crane that served as conclusion to his major critical book *In Defense of Reason,* and for that reason they might have been set aside from the bulk of his correspondence. Winters, however, took a proprietary interest in the letters from Crane. When Crane's mother wrote to him after Crane's death, he warned her about the dangers of publishing an inadequate book and urged her to consult with Allen Tate. She did not answer him. At the time Winters thought of editing and annotating the letters for *Symposium,* but it looked to him like a big job that he could not undertake for a year or two. He was reluctant to turn them over to the Crane estate and unwilling to undertake their publication. Writing to Tate he said that he had a few important letters, much understating what he had at hand. Years later when Brom Weber was editing the letters of Crane he put off Weber's inquiries and implied that he had burned the letters. They remained in his study for about five years after his death until Janet Lewis Winters found them as she was going through his library. There will always be an aura of mystery about this episode in our literary history, but at least the letters exist. My best efforts have not

located Winters's letters to Crane, but his contemporaneous letters to Allen Tate have served to fill in gaps and show how Winters wrote to his poetic colleagues. Crane may have destroyed the
letters from Winters in irritation at his review of *The Bridge* or
they may have been lost during his wanderings or they may yet
show up. If they do, as indicated above, they could not be published until 1993. The importance of Crane's letters to Winters
seems to me great enough to warrant doing the best possible at
present.

In treating the difficult problem of presenting a correspondence between two vigorous and temperamental persons when
only one voice can be directly presented, I have tried to refrain
from constructing Winters's part in the correspondence on opinion and guess. I have relied mainly on interviews with Janet Lewis
Winters, Winters's letters to Allen Tate, Winters's published
work, and the internal evidence of Crane's letters to Winters.
John Unterecker's *Voyager, A Life of Hart Crane* was a steady
source of information as was Brom Weber's edition of *The Letters of Hart Crane*. I have avoided such phrases as "It is highly
probable that . . ." or "It is almost certain that . . ." because the
entire text deals with the almost certain and the highly probable,
especially when treating Winters's side of the correspondence.

Living with the problems posed by the correspondence brought
the poetry of the two men back to my close attention, and that
was a genuine reward. Crane and Winters were remarkable poets,
and their work stands out even among the substantial inventive-
ness, originality, and accomplishment of American poetry from
1912 on. Crane's brilliance has long been celebrated, and Winters's poetry, while less commented upon than Crane's, has had
devoted advocates. His poetry is a rich and various body of work,
and its merit has been partly obscured by Winters's commanding
reputation as a critic. But Winters thought of himself as primarily a poet, his criticism being ancillary to the poetic labor.
During his lifetime he published over three hundred lyric poems.
His criticism grew from and enriched his poetry, and he also felt
obliged to point out historical and philosophical confusions in
current literary thought.

His poetic reputation has been further clouded by his own treatment of his early work. Until the publication of his collected *Early Poems* in 1966, his large body of experimental free verse was practically inaccessible, so that the range of his accomplishment was known only to relatively few readers. In his early style he developed a lucid rigorous free verse and took aspects of modern experimentalism much farther than anyone else had. Eventually, he found that style not adequate to his experience and ambitions, so that from 1928 on he wrote in more conventionally measured lines. In both modes he wrote very well indeed, and one reason for the quality of his later work is the discipline developed in his experimental period. At his best, he had technical expertise that is the envy and admiration of other poets. Robert Lowell had unqualified praise for Winters's *Collected Poems:*

> Winters likes to declare himself a classicist. Dimwits have called him a conservative. He was the kind of conservative who was so original and radical that his poems were never reprinted in the anthologies for almost twenty years. Neither the *avant-garde* nor the vulgar had an eye for him. He was a poet so solitary that he was praised adequately only by his pupils and by Allen Tate. Yet Winters is a writer of great passion, one of the most steady rhetoricians in the language, and a stylist whose diction and metric exemplify two hundred years of American culture.[7]

When Winters wrote at the peak of his powers, each poem was a densely complicated structure, embodying passionate intellect. The main preoccupation of the work is with the relation between intelligence and feeling, the mystery and inevitability of death, the falseness of purity and the deceptions of experience, the dangers of greed and other unrestrained passions, the powers and limits of mind and will. They are deeply serious poems, and they have an air of completeness, so that even poems on a common theme printed in sequence are self-contained and closed off from one another. Each poem seems isolated, so that the work does not immediately appear as a body of interconnecting and mutually

enriching forms. Winters is a poet concerned with ethical problems, but he is not primarily didactic. He trusted the poem and
not the asserted idea or judgment, so that his main concern was
with fully realized experience rather than with any system. The
poetic took precedence over the metaphysical or any systematic
ethic.

This accounts for the response that each poem is a new start;
even with the poems on the frontier, or the poems on the trial of
David Lamson, or the poems on classical myths, Winters seems
deliberately to establish with each poem a fresh set of poetic problems to explore and satisfy. The mark of Winters is present in
each of the poems, there is individual style, but the appeal is not
to the style or general point of view. If Winters's poetic method
has unfortunate results, they appear on occasions when discipline
becomes constraint, when formalism seems to be an end in itself,
and when feeling is so deliberately thwarted that the poem becomes unnaturally dry. The poet's willful intent then seems the
only reason for the poem's existence; this is often true with the
brief occasional poems. But there are many fine poems by Winters, both in his experimental and his traditional periods. For
many readers, the best ingress would be the poems on the frontier, "John Day, Frontiersman," "John Sutter," "The California
Oaks," "On Rereading a Passage from John Muir," and "The
Manzanita," where Winters is at his most proficient and lucid,
and where the emotional overtones are rich and complicated.

The contrast with Crane is instructive. Crane also wanted to
write autonomous poems, as he often did. But he permitted himself greater emotional freedom, and he took large chances, not
always with happy results.

Crane is capable of grossness and banality and sentimentality
that Winters would never permit himself. He is often obscure on
principle because he persistently violates the limits of language.
What saves him is precisely what Winters lacks, the lift and excitement of movement from poem to poem, the sense that something has been promised but not realized, that the realization is
potentially there and may come to pass at any moment, so that all
will become harmonious and clear. There are few resting points

where all is drawn together. The metaphors and diction are distracting, and what concentrations occur are brief and limited. One remembers lines and passages and here and there an entire poem. The poems communicate the sense of an ongoing poetic life rather than an enterprise, and the appeal is to an antecedent experience rather than one contained and finished. That experience is excited, undifferentiated, and the style is appropriately exclamatory. Crane reaches through his language toward a reality that it may create. The effort is bold to the point of danger, the danger that all may collapse.

And yet there is a genuine attractiveness in Crane's poetry, partly in its texture and partly in the very sense of risk and imminent collapse that complements the sense of hope and trust that takes one from line to line and poem to poem. So powerful a rhetoric may reflect and create a new world. Beyond the merely poetic rests the interest of the person. Dead at thirty-three, he required a biography of 773 pages, and shortly after its publication an edition of the Crane family letters appeared with over 600 pages of text. Although much of the interest in his life wavers between the romantic and the prurient, the fact remains that Crane in his life and work has become a symbolic figure. His first biographer chose as subtitle a phrase that was prophetic: "The Life of an American Poet." No one would claim that Crane was a typical American poet, but he has—as Winters also prophesied—become a tragic symbol.

I find it useless to act as if the poetry could be considered aside from the life of Crane. He was energetic, intelligent, and often charming. He was also, whether reluctant or not, an extremely unhappy homosexual. His drinking was massive and self-destructive, and his relations with his family troubled and almost allegorical in their implications, whether artistic, commercial, or sexual. His life drove him to all excesses including the ultimate excess of suicide. The tale is as terrible as his talent was great, and it is inescapable.

There are no simple terms that cover the remarkable poetic abilities of these two men, but it does seem to me that these letters and the ancillary material pertinent to their work and their lives grant a fresh perspective on both of them that may help us to see not only them but ourselves and the art of poetry in America with some of the clichés disturbed if not destroyed. Crane and Winters are complementary types, certainly among the great talents of American literature, both of them in some way incomplete, obsessed men. In this book I have tried to maintain some feeling of justice in treating them because of the importance I place on their poetry and their sense of life. They have instructed me; it has been a great pleasure to enter this unknown area of the poetic consciousness.

I

A MEETING OF MINDS

In the fall of 1926 Yvor Winters began his second year of teaching at the University of Idaho in Moscow. His work included several courses in elementary French and one course in Contemporary French Literature. He found Moscow very dull, without entertainment, intellectual conversation, or anything like a poetic community. He was already, at the age of twenty-six, fairly well known as a poet, and he had prepared himself for teaching by intensive study at the University of Colorado, concentrating in Romance Languages with a minor in Latin.

Moscow was a town of about 5,000, set in a bleak landscape with a severe climate. Winters's isolation was relieved by the presence of two of his Airedales, one with a broken leg who had to be carried in and out of the house. Although Winters had married Janet Lewis in summer, she was unable to accompany him and remained under treatment for tuberculosis at Sunmount Sanatorium near Santa Fe. They corresponded, and he extended his knowledge of Romance Languages by studying Portuguese. He prepared his third book of poems for publication, and he read contemporary little magazines, *Poetry, The Little Review, The Dial,* whatever came to his attention that he could afford. He was not only supporting himself on the meager pay of an instructor but paying Janet Lewis's bills at the sanatorium. His life was frugal and austere, devoted to poetry and a heavy teaching load. He was solitary and lonely.

In October of 1926 he picked up his mail one day and found in
it one letter from Allen Tate and another from Hart Crane. The
letter from Tate brought the news of Crane's harrowing experience with the hurricane at the Isle of Pines and asked Winters
whether he had any poems to contribute to an anthology, one of
several abortive enterprises that Tate started in those days. Winters sent him some poems and apologized for not having read any
of Tate's work, though he had heard good things about it. He also
wondered whether Tate shared Crane's aversion to William Carlos Williams. Williams was much on Winters's mind, not only because of the objective value of the poetry but because he thought
of himself as an imagist, was in fact writing experimental poems
in a line parallel to and strikingly different from the free verse line
of Williams. He had also published a long essay on the mechanics
of the poetic image, "The Testament of a Stone," which occupied
an entire issue of *Secession*. The essay was central to his thought.
He revised it and made it part of his Master's thesis at Colorado
and with further slight revisions he included it in his 1934 doctoral
dissertation at Stanford. In Moscow he was busily translating it
into French at the suggestion of Frank Schoell and René Lalou.

Winters initiated the correspondence with Tate, and he was
grateful for it, as he was to receive Crane's letters. They con-
nected him with the larger literary world and made Moscow more
habitable. His continued interest in French poetry had led him to
compile an anthology from Leconte de Lisle to Radiguet as sub-
stantiation of his argument. He was, at that time, planning eventually to study French literature in Paris. A career as professor of
English was far from his mind.

He was a poet and a student of poetry, and that would be his
life's work. He was born in Chicago on October 17, 1900, but unlike the other literary figures whose lives marched with the century, he was, from the perspective of New York or Paris, the unseen man of American letters. When he was quite young his family moved to Eagle Rock, near Pasadena, and he spent his childhood in those as yet unspoiled hills. Eagle Rock has now melted
indistinguishably into Los Angeles, but at the time they were
occupying one of a half dozen or so houses in what was a very

beautiful area. His family moved to Seattle briefly, and then returned to Chicago where his father was a stock and grain broker for Thomson and McKinnon. They lived comfortably, but the myth that Winters never had to worry about anything because his father was a rich stockbroker is precisely that, a myth. He went to tough schools and found it necessary to learn how to defend himself, so that he took up boxing and became rather good at it until a heart strain—athlete's heart, as it is called—forced him to give it up. In his adolescence he became deeply interested in biology, was a member of the Illinois Microscopical Society and a devotée of the writings of Jacques Loeb, a biochemist with a strict mechanical interpretation of natural phenomena. His serious interest in poetry began at the age of fourteen, and he read contemporary poetry with close attention. He lived in the age of little magazines, and at sixteen he began his subscription to *Poetry: A Magazine of Verse,* as well as gathering what copies he could of *The Little Review* and *Others.* He also began a library of books by Yeats, Pound, Williams, and other modern poets. Like many readers, epspecially younger ones, he knew Stevens's work and loved it before the 1923 publication of *Harmonium.* In 1917 he entered the University of Chicago and joined the Poetry Club, where he met Glenway Wescott and Elizabeth Roberts. Through the club he met Harriet Monroe, who encouraged him to visit her in her office. There he read back issues of *Poetry* and books in her considerable collection of modern poetry and criticism. She was very kind to him, and when tuberculosis forced him to leave Chicago in the winter of 1918 she gave him issues of *Poetry* which filled the early gaps in his collection.

He left Chicago for Pasadena, where he stayed only briefly, and then went to Sunmount Sanatorium near Santa Fe, where he was to spend three years as a patient. He had his files of *Poetry,* subscriptions to *Others* and *The Little Review,* and subscribed to or purchased additional magazines as they came to his attention. Alice Corbin Henderson was also at Sunmount, and Winters's father gave Glenway Wescott a subsidy so that he could live in Santa Fe and give Winters congenial literary conversation. The years at Sunmount were not entirely isolated, though patients lived in separate cottages and were enjoined to spend most of their time in bed. The disease was enervating, as Winters's memory of his experience indicated:

> The patient was often allowed, or even encouraged, to exercise; the only known cure, and this was known to only a few physicians, was absolute rest, often immobilized rest. The disease filled the body with a fatigue so heavy that it was an acute pain, pervasive and poisonous.[1]

Even in such a condition, Winters persevered in the writing of verse, and his first published poems appeared in 1919, three in *Youth* and six in *Poetry*. His first book, *The Immobile Wind*, and most of his second, *The Magpie's Shadow*, were written at Sunmount. During those years, the height and spring of youth, Winters lived in the face of death and in isolation, and he did so with courage and will and dignity.

Toward the end of his stay at Sunmount, Winters had a serious dispute with his parents, who wanted him to break off associations with some of his friends in Santa Fe. Winters refused, and when released from the sanatorium in 1921, he was on his own financially. He visited Chicago briefly, where he first met Janet Lewis. He then returned to the Santa Fe area where he had a job teaching grade school at Madrid, twenty miles to the southwest of Santa Fe. In 1922 Janet Lewis was forced by her health to go to Sunmount, and in the fall Winters taught secondary school at Los Cerrillos. Two touching vignettes survive from his students in that remote, violent, and poverty-stricken milieu. By spring of 1923 he had made peace with his family, and they gave him financial support to attend the University of Colorado. He went for nine consecutive terms, including summers.

His most intent studies were in French, Spanish, and Latin, and his work was very good, in the high 80s and 90s, except in some general requirements in history and psychology, though his grades only once fell below 80. He received a 75 in a course in principles of teaching. Practice was Winters's strong point.

One amusing episode occurred during those two years. A young man who wrote verse and admired Winters immensely was also busy in clear-cutting the virgins of Boulder. He was once called before the dean because he had announced publicly that no female English major was a virgin, to his certain knowledge. He assumed that for a poet a reputation as sexual athlete could bring nothing but good, so he spread a rumor that Winters lived on the outskirts of town because he was keeping a mistress.

In fact, Winters was living on the outskirts of town because it was cheaper. He sent part of his small allowance to Elizabeth Madox Roberts to help her through an illness, and he needed room for his three Airedales, to exercise them, and to keep their barking from irritating neighbors. Winters always thought that this gleeful spreading of rumors rather quashed his chances at Boulder.

He received the degree of Master of Arts on August 29, 1925. His thesis was *A Method of Critical Approach to Works of Literature Based Primarily Upon a Study of the Lyric in French and English.* It was ninety pages in length, about a third of it taken up by "The Testament of a Stone" in a new version, the remainder by discussions of some of the ideas that would later form parts of his doctoral dissertation and his first critical book *Primitivism and Decadence.* The stress is on contemporary American poets, notably Marianne Moore, Eliot, Pound, Stevens, and Williams. The result is a curiously disjointed document, concluding with a series of brief notes on poetic problems. With the degree granted late in August, he was then on his way to Moscow, Idaho, armed with the ability to read and write Spanish and French and with a good Latin background. As he ruefully noted much later, his abilities did not include the capacity to speak French or Spanish.

I have given so full an accounting of Winters's early years because until the "Introduction" to *The Early Poems of Yvor Winters,* appeared in 1966, very little knowledge of his early years was publicly available.[2] Janet Lewis Winters has provided some details, and the letters to Allen Tate have added others.[3] Winters was an important man in the world of letters, and the deference paid to him by Crane was not excessive. Winters at the age of twenty-six was a learned man, a poet with a growing reputation, and through his correspondence and reviews a man with evident

critical powers. His work had been extensively published in little
magazines, *Poetry, Forge, 1924, The Dial, Broom, Secession,
Voices, This Quarter,* and it was in the little magazines that
poetic reputations in that period were made. Stevens and Crane
were both well known before their first books were collected and
published, and Crane and Tate read not Winters's two pamphlets
but individual poems and groups of poems in magazines. The
pamphlets he would send to them, though he had gone well past
the work done at Sunmount by the time they started their correspondence.

Winters also knew Harriet Monroe, and he had corresponded
extensively with Marianne Moore—she had sent him books from
her vantage point at the New York Public Library while he was
teaching in New Mexico, and she had published several of his
poems in *The Dial* and one review. Monroe and Moore were cita-
dels to be stormed, and Crane looked on Winters as a potential
ally.

The story of Crane's life has been told often and at length. It
was outwardly more dramatic and eventful than Winters's, and
his bizarre conduct and excesses have inevitably been the center
of discussion and speculation. His relations with Winters compose
an unwritten chapter in his work and thought.

Part of that chapter has been written. Crane was, as Winters
insisted, very intelligent. He was also extremely generous when
his deepest personal and poetic concerns were engaged. Malcolm
Cowley has written about Crane's selflessness in a full and particular way. Crane insisted that Cowley had a book of poems, and
he went about the process of forcing that book into publication.
He edited and typed a manuscript for Cowley, and he got a publisher. Later Cowley would choose a different publisher and prepare a different ordering of the poems. He never denied his debt
to Crane. Cowley expressed his sense of indebtedness clearly:

> As I piece together the story now, with a renewed feeling of
> gratitude to Hart, I think again how different he was in spirit
> from the drunken rioter he is often pictured as being. All this

took place in the period of his noisiest riots, and yet he devoted sober weeks to editing and typing and peddling the manuscript of a friend. He was absolutely lacking in professional jealousy, except toward T. S. Eliot, and that was a compliment to Eliot; otherwise Hart was jealous only of the great dead.[4]

Crane's poetic spirit and his critical intelligence have been too little noted, except in such comments as Cowley's, and his relations with Winters show that spirit and intelligence at work.

From the beginning, Crane was grateful for Winters's interest in his work, and he showed a lively appreciation of the poems that Winters sent him. He was impressed by Winters's systematic knowledge of Romance languages, and even endowed him with a knowledge of Greek which Winters did not have. The correspondence began while Crane was living on the Isle of Pines, and Winters's letters were especially welcome not only because of their appreciation of his poetry but because they diminished his loneliness. In spite of the jovial tolerant companship of the housekeeper Mrs. T. W. Simpson, the "Aunt Sally" referred to in his letters and in "The River" section of *The Bridge,* he was living in literary and intellectual solitude. He had gone to the island after a fierce but trivially motivated quarrel with Allen Tate and Caroline Gordon had made further residence with them at Patterson impossible. Later they would all think of the incident as laughable, but it did not seem funny at the time.

Waldo Frank accompanied him to the island and spent a few weeks with him before returning to New York, but otherwise the period from early May through October was accented only by letters from Frank and other friends, annoying letters and equally upsetting silences from his mother, and what was to be the last continuously productive period of his poetic life. One benefit of solitude was that he drank very little, mainly because, as he ruefully observed, there was nobody to drink with. But he did have in July and August a great outburst of productive work, resulting in the bulk of *The Bridge* and several incidental poems. He knew ecstasy in that experience, and he was further encouraged by the certainty that *White Buildings* would soon be published, with Allen Tate's generous introduction made even more precious by the capacity for selflessness it exhibited.

Still, he was enervated by the Caribbean heat and as always troubled by his precarious financial position. Even before a hurricane hit the island in the third week of October, he had planned to leave. With the house in ruins, the only alternative was a return to Patterson, though not to live with the Tates. This brought him closer to the troubles of his parents, so that he was nagged by a sense of guilt and inadequacy. His father's second wife was dying painfully and surely of cancer; his mother was going through an unpleasant divorce from her second husband; his grandmother was in ill health. The return from the Isle of Pines to Patterson brought him closer to his friends in the immediate vicinity and in New York City. But Patterson in winter was cold and isolated, New York was hectic, and news from Cleveland brought a tone of gloom approaching despair.

Very little of this comes through Crane's letters to Winters, and I suspect that very little sense of Winters's loneliness appeared in his letters. Although only one of Winters's letters to Crane, and that one trivial, has survived, he was writing extensively to Allen Tate at the same time, and my belief is that those letters parallel the ones to Crane in their insistent concentration on problems of poetic practice and theory.

Crane's first letter to Winters has an ebullient tone, partly because of the euphoria that remained from his creative activity, and partly in gratitude for Winters's high estimate of the merit of Crane's "For the Marriage of Faustus and Helen." The judgments from the remote quarter of Idaho had special weight, being objective and not, as many favorable commentaries on his work did, coming from close personal acquaintanceship. During Crane's argument with Harriet Monroe over the metaphors of "At Melville's Tomb," Winters had written in support of Crane, and Harriet Monroe had quoted his statement that "For the Marriage of Faustus . . . seems to me one of the great poems of our time — as great as the best of Stevens or Pound or Eliot."[5] In the same letter (dated May 11, 1926) Winters had urged her to print Crane because he wrote well, at least not jingles. Crane very rightly considered Winters an ally.

It seems strange, in view of later developments, to find Crane adducing Whitman as part of the base that he and Winters shared, but at the time Winters had not come to his settled bias against Whitman. Soon he would be reading the poetry of Emerson with such admiration that he placed him in the category of Emily Dickinson, establishing an American tradition that to his mind went from Emerson to Dickinson to Williams and Crane. Winters in 1926 had some strong personal opinions on poetry, but he had not arrived at any systematic sense of the traditions of poetry in English. He did share Crane's dislike of Sandburg and his admiration for Frost, and he was eager to convert Crane to liking Williams: Williams was for him both a passion and a model. He could not take Crane's dismissal of him lightly.

Winters in his letter evidently proposed an exchange of manuscripts. He was at the time engaged in translating from French and Spanish as well as in preparing *The Bare Hills* for its ultimate publication in 1927. Crane, after his writing binge of the summer, had most of *The Bridge* completed while lacking the energy to make fresh copies of the finished passages. The Isle of Pines was undermining his will, especially the heat and the endless mosquitoes (the "squeks" of the letter).

When he turned to the literary scene, Crane had a grievance against Marianne Moore. Because she so thoroughly rewrote his "The Wine Menagerie" that the changes are indescribable, it seems wise to reproduce here the version that appeared in *The Dial* for May 1926 so that it can be compared with Crane's original version, which is readily available in Crane's *Complete Poems*.[6]

Again

by Hart Crane

What in this heap in which the serpent pries,
Reflects the sapphire transepts round the eyes—

The angled octagon upon a skin,
Facsimile of time unskeined,
From which some whispered carillon assures
Speed to the arrow into feathered skies?

New thresholds, new anatomies,
New freedoms now distil
This competence, to travel in a tear,
Sparkling alone within another's will.

My blood dreams a receptive smile
Wherein new purities are snared. There chimes
Before some flame a restless shell
Tolled once perhaps by every tongue in hell.
Anguished the wit cries out of me, "The world
Has followed you. Though in the end you know
And count some dim inheritance of sand,
How much yet meets the treason of the snow."

Whatever the faults and merits of the original version, they were at least Crane's. In this version, praise and blame to to Marianne Moore. When Crane says that "Repose of Rivers" escaped her clutches, he simply means that she did not rewrite the poem; it and other works by Crane continued to be printed in *The Dial.* "Repose of Rivers" appeared in *The Dial* in pages immediately preceding Anthony Wrynn's "Where This River Ends." Wrynn was an architect and friend of Winters from his days in Santa Fe.

In the letter it is a little surprising that Crane did not recognize Ernest Walsh, the editor of *This Quarter,* a very fine magazine that published both Winters's and Crane's friend Isidore Schneider. Winters held it up to Harriet Monroe as a model of what a literary magazine should be. Elbert Hubbard is not arbitrarily chosen — Crane's father once, in one of his moments of goodwill that merely underlined his failure to understand his son, apprenticed him to Hubbard, who ran a literary factory of uplift and self-service. Crane left quickly in disgust. Hubbard is chiefly re-

membered as the author of *A Message to Garcia* and for his brief
relations with Hart Crane and Stephen Crane. Kay Boyle was a
contributor to *This Quarter* and a close friend to Walsh.

                                          Box 1373
                                          Nueva Gerona
                                          Isle of Pines, Cuba
                                          Oct. 5th, 1926

Dear Yvor Winters:
   It is just a 10-to-1 accident that I didn't write you first. What
little of your work I have occasionally seen has stuck in my mind
— as little else I see does. And I was recently so grateful to you for
what was quoted to me as your opinion of "Faustus & Helen" (I
refer to the current correspondence between Aunt Harriet and
me, printed in "Poetry") that I was restrained only by the fear of
immodesty.
   I think that the scene, so far as poetry goes, has never been
quite so clouded as right now. In many ways, it would be much
better if so many people weren't even mildly interested in
"poetry." We have had the scullery permutations of Amy Lowell,
and the batter bakes thick and heavy even on the charcoal
embers! Sometime in the saturnalian past Elbert Hubbard found
the ghost of Harriet Beecher Stowe, and on a slab of the sunburnt
West they managed to conceive Carl Sandburg, a tiresome half-
way person, even though a poet. (I am trying to wade through all
the homespun crinoline of his recent and much lauded "Lincoln,"
but find I'd almost prefer some coldhearted academic treatise
without so much wet dreaming on Nancy Hanks, daisies and
prairie prostrations: "milk-sick" is a word that often occurs, and
too symbolically, I fear.) One goes back to Poe, and to Whitman
— and always my beloved Melville — with renewed appreciation of
what America really is, or could be. And one may go back to
Frost with the same certainty, — a good, clean artist, however
lean. Cummings (at times) and Marianne Moore, too. As you say,

Williams can shed his shirt, —but I think he is too much a quick-change artist. His specialty is both hair-shirting and war-whooping: never more than constant experimentation. There are some things that are certain, after all, Kit Marlowe is one kind, and Mencken is another.

Miss Moore's paces are stubborn, and once, in my case destructive. "Repose of Rivers" escaped her clutches successfully, as most everything else of mine published henceforth. But that frightful "Again" (what she must have said with lifted brows and a ? mark when she opened the envelope) was the wreck of a longer and entirely different poem "The Wine Menagerie" which I hope you will see in its original nudity when my book, "White Buildings," comes out from Boni & Liveright sometime around December. I was *obliged* to submit to her changes, not only because I was penniless at the time but because I owed money to others at the time equally penniless. When I saw that senseless thing in print I almost wept.

The "new Metaphysics" that Whitman proclaimed in "Democratic Vistas" is evident here and there in America today. I feel it in your work, and I think I can sense it in some of my own work. (Probably Whitman wouldn't recognize it in either of us, but no matter). That *sine qua non* evidently has to be fought for and defended. I'm doing my best about it here and now, fighting off miasmas, bugs, hay fever, bats and tropical squeks and birds— toward "The Bridge" a very long poem for these days, extending from Columbus to Brooklyn Bridge and Atlantis. It is three-fourths done, and I may have to flee the torments (now settled in my nerves) to New Orleans soon to finish it. It will be a book by itself. And in it I shall incidentally try to answer all my friends who have for three years, now, sat down and complacently joined the monotonous choruses of "The Waste Land." (The Dedication to it you may soon see in *The Dial*).

These preoccupations make me an inactive enthusiast toward the sensible proposals you make in your letter to me. I simply haven't time to copy out anything, nor extra energy. But I have more than time and energy to read anything of yours that you'll be kind and patient enough to send me. Won't you do so, saving such things as translations until later'? Another admirer of yours, Allen Tate, RFD, Patterson, NYork, might be more energetic. I'm sure he would be glad to hear from you about the matter, anyway. I don't recall anything whatever about "Walsh," whom you refer to. I have never met Wrynn, but I am distinctly grateful to him for the story in the last *Dial,* especially the very beautiful close of it. Kay Boyle's stuff has always seems a kind of diluted solution of some kind. She's still in France, n'est-ce-pas?

I don't mean to bluster on forever. But do write me again — with the proper enclosures! And thank you for your letter. Present address is good regardless of what changes ensue. Please offer my salutations to Janet Lewis.

> *Yours most faithfully,*
> *Hart Crane*

Within a very few days, Crane had recovered his energies to such an extent that he could make a copy of the "Cutty Sark" section of *The Bridge.* Winters enjoyed it immensely, though he was puzzled by the names of the ships. Crane could not have meant that the third page was a calligram in the sense that it produced the kind of image that marks Apollinaire's *Calligrammes.* He simply wanted the lineation to mark clearly the movement of the language, rather than shape, for instance, the rigging of a ship, as Apollinaire's poems give the visual image of a heart.

Although Crane may have relied on more than one book for his sources in the latter part of the poem, his chief reference was Basil Lubbock's *The China Clippers,*[7] which has brief descriptions of the loss of *Ariel* (disappeared 1872) and *Taeping* (lost on a reef in the same year). The closing appeals of the poem are thus to two ghosts. Of the ships mentioned by Crane, only *Nimbus* is not treated in Lubbock's text, and it may have come from another book or — more likely — have been invented by Crane.

It is gratifying that Crane should have had fun with this poem.

Winters in his 1930 review of *The Bridge* singled it out for praise:

> *Cutty Sark* is a frail but exquisite and almost incompara-
> bly skillful dance of shadows. Its conclusion is a perpetual
> delight.[8]

This was the first section of *The Bridge* which Winters was to see.
It differs somewhat from the final version. Two of the ships bear
other names: *Flying Cloud* was originally *Flying Spur*; *Rainbow*
was *Chrysolite* (all in Lubbock). There was no mention of Atlantis in this early version, and punctuation and diction differed.
Essentially, however, the poem was parallel to the finished version.

Box 1373
Nueva Gerona
Isle of Pines, Cuba
Oct. 9th, 1926

Dear Yvor Winters:
    I'm enclosing a carbon of one of the middle sections of "The
Bridge." It may interest you.
    The punctuation, or rather lack of it, is intended to present the
endless continuum of water motion, with the rather "grailish"
Atlantis-Rose theme acting as a kind of fugue counterpoint.
Third page is pure calligramme, and I shan't allow it to be
printed in any detail other than the mss designates, — line-end
word divisions and all have an organic purpose. I can't resist saying that I have got more fun out of this little "regatta" than
almost any poem I ever wrote.
    When you have time let me know what you think of it, frankly,
of course. I'm hoping for some of yours soon.

Cordially,
Hart Crane

By October 28, Crane was back in New York, driven there by a hurricane that had effectively demolished his house. Winters had initiated his correspondence with Tate by writing to inquire about Crane's well-being, and Crane hastened to reassure him.

New York
Nov. 1

Dear Winters:

Tate tells me that you have been anxious about me since the hurricane: well, I got it, full force, and just escaped without a fever. Ghastly before it, worse after!

Am terribly rushed and undecided as yet as to exactly where I shall settle. But write me RFD—Patterson, New York, wherefrom mail will be forwarded, whether I settle there or not. I fully expect to get (eventually) whatever you may have written me on the Island.

With my best to you,
Hart Crane

Once settled in Patterson under the protective affectionate wing of Mrs. Turner, Crane could turn to literary questions. Winters had pursued further the question of Williams's accomplishment, and Crane conceded the value of some poems. Winters's instigation led him to read *In the American Grain,* as a letter of November 21 to Waldo Frank indicates. Crane was not alone in having Williams pressed upon him by Winters. At about the same time, Winters was praising *In the American Grain* as superior to *Ulysses* and Elizabeth Madox Roberts's *The Time of Man* to Allen Tate and asserting that he had spent five years in trying to undermine Williams on theoretical grounds, only to find that it could not be done. He compared Williams favorably to Hardy, Arnold, Dickinson, Browning, and Corbière; at times he seemed to attain the level of Baudelaire and Rimbaud. What most irritated him was the attention paid to Cummings at the expense of Williams.

Patterson, New York
Rural Delivery
November 12th

Dear Winters:

Although the hurricane experience (and engineering my way off the Island afterward) were strenuous experiences, it is the previous heat and subsequent chaos of worries and details and travel which, I believe, account for my present vacant state of mind. At any rate, this may partially serve as an excuse for the present dullard answer to your very pleasant letter just arrived here via the Isle of Pines. I'll probably recover myself better later on; meanwhile I greatly appreciate your interest in a number of ways.

I am back where I started from last May, a farmhouse with an old woman to cook for me. It seems good to "experience" nights again—not filled with the overweening, obscene vitality of the tropics which never lets you (a northerner) rest. And though fate seems to throw me into sudden extremes, winters in polar regions and summers under the equator, I can at least hope to rest up a little, i.e. if I am not yanked off to Cleveland on account of growing difficulties there, where my family is immersed in sickness, etc. The above address will always be good, however, as I maintain a room here permanently for a few personal belongings. Letters are quickly forwarded.

Your suggestion regarding the instructorship would certainly interest me very much were I at all equipped to respond. I'm not being merely modest when I say that my French is weak and my Spanish nil. I've never been through high-school, even. So you can see what a splurge I'd create! I always envy people like yourself—their entry into pages I shall never see. . . . And, after all, your isolation and work is much pleasanter than newspaper reporting and ad-writing, such as I've been raised on.

The Aunt Harriet harangue makes an interesting story. What gave her any initial impetus toward taste or selection was immediately withdrawn when Pound stopped sending her lectures and material. Now she is back on the ancient journalistic footing where he found her. Her "position" and excessive self-confidence, however, will never forsake her. She is the kind of person who would run up to Newton, and in behalf of all good easy-going "hopefuls" of the middle-west, would query, "But aren't you a little bit too mathematical, Sir Isaac?" There is good antidote for the kind of criticism she writes in Edwin Muir's last book, "Transition." You may have already seen it; I like especially his treatment of Eliot and Joyce. He is the only one I've read who touches the real weakness both in Eliot's poetry and criticism.

My reference to Williams's work did me no more justice than him, it was too hasty to be representative. I have not read all the poems that you mention of his, but I've read about two-thirds of them. Some of them are truly unforgettable, especially the Postlude. And I remember a suite published once in the *Little Review* called To Mark Antony in heaven. . . . Or was it a single poem? I have *Sour Grapes,* and had *Spring and All*. . .until the hurricane. I don't want to read *In the American Grain* until I get through with Bridge because I hesitate to complicate the organization of a work, which, from what I've heard of his chronicle, is on such similar subject matter. Certainly Williams is brilliant, and occasionally profound. Full of clean recognitions and discoveries. And I like Williams personally.

I am eagerly awaiting your poems, the mss. your letter promised. If they get lost on the way back through Havana post office I shall be much disappointed. At any rate the mss. of your book had probably not been sent to that address before the storm. Your expressed esteem for certain of my poems makes me doubly anxious that *White Buildings*—in regard to such work as you haven't seen—will entertain and please you. It ought to be out in about two weeks.

Faithfully yours,
Hart Crane

By November 15, Crane had received letters forwarded from the Isle of Pines, and he felt compelled to write in appreciation. Flattery?—there was some of that, but more important is a kind of release, the recognition that finally he has found someone with a direct perception of what his poetry was driving toward. His feelings of gratitude toward this complete stranger who, purely on the basis of his poetry, was trying to get him jobs and offering financial aid, grew cumulatively. He could write to Winters freely and with trust that he would be understood. The initial quotation comes from Winters's description of the basic component of poetic art, whether metaphor in Crane's sense of the matter or image in Winters's. The phrase appears in Winters's poem "To the Painter Polelonema" in slightly different form. After describing the energetic activity of the painting, the way in which Polelonema could wring life from rock and through intelligent love penetrate external nature, the poem concludes:

> No sparrow
> cracks these seeds
>
> that no wind blows.

In his letter Winters was speaking of the irreducible quality of Crane's metaphors, their resistance to the kind of analysis that Harriet Monroe and others imposed upon them.

Winters by this time had the "Ave Maria" segment of *The Bridge* before him. The version Winters had was entitled "San Cristobal," and Crane had made the mistake of spelling *Madre* as *Madra* and stressing *laudamus* on the first syllable. Eventually these were corrected. There are detailed differences between this and the final version; they are important but not substantive.

Perhaps most important in this letter is Crane's brief explanation of what a "bridge" and therefore *the* bridge might mean: the annihilation of space and time, the essential unity of all realities beyond appearance. Such bridging goes beyond logic to dream and metaphor. Meditating on these problems, Crane prefigures the judgments that would see the poem as a magnificent failure, or as he here phrases it, "...the kind of half-success that is worse than failure."

Patterson, New York
Nov. 15. '26

Dear Yvor Winters:

"—seeds that no sparrow will ever crack"—!

I feel almost like shouting *Eureka!* Your letter of Oct. 20th has just reached me from the Island. And I must thank you for the most intimate sort of critical sympathy—not only with my work, but my aims—that I've about ever been given. I am convinced now that telepathy is constantly at work, for I have, I confess it now, been so impressed by a certain kinship in certain stray poems I have seen of yours at wide intervals—that I have thought at times, when pausing over certain lines of my own, —"well, Winters, I think, would like this line." But one scarcely dares expect such explicitness as yours in locating and justifying that code of reference, that metaphysical common denominator upon which our composite values seem to rest. We may differ in many a detail, but I'm amazed at our essential sympathy. (You see, it's most pleasant to find someone who (regardless of whether he wants to crack them or not) values the hard little kernels (really bombs) which most other people blame you for having "spoiled" the "clarity" of your work with, —especially when these kernels are (to me) the *élan-vital* of the poem!)

Your quotations are, several of them, old favorites of mine. And you are right about modern epics—except—until somebody actually overcomes the limitations. This will have to be done by a new form, —and of course, new forms are never desirable until they are simply forced into being by new materials. Perhaps any modern equivalent of the old epic form should be called by some other name, for certainly, as I see it, the old definition cannot cover the kind of poem I am trying to write except on certain fundamental points. At least both are concerned with material which can be called mythical.... But what is "mythical" in or

rather, of the twentieth century is not the Kaiser, the sinking of
the Titanic, etc. Rather is it science, travel, (in the sense of speed)
—psychoanalysis, etc. With, of course, the eternal verities of sea,
mountain and river still at work.

The old narrative form, then, —with its concomitant species of
rhetoric, is obviously unequal to the task. It may well be that the
link-by-link cumulative effect of the ancients cannot have an
equivalent in any modern epic form. However, there are certain
basically mythical factors in our Western world which literally cry
for embodiment. Oddly, as I see it, they cannot be presented
completely (any one of them) in isolated order, but in order to
appear in their true, luminous reality must be presented in chron-
ological and organic order, out of which you get a kind of bridge,
the quest of which bridge is—nothing less ambitious than the
annihilation of time and space, the prime myth of the modern
world.

The labor in locating the interrelations between sources, facts
and appearances in all this is, believe me, difficult. One may be
doomed to the kind of half-success which is worse than failure. I
could write reams in regard to certain startling discoveries made
along the way, simply in trying to handle my subject in an organic
way. One of them is the currency of Indian symbolism in whatever is most real in our little native culture, its persistence, despite
our really slight contact with that race, into architecture, painting, etc. —cropping out in the most unexpected places.

> A cyclone threshes in the turbine crest,
> Swooping in eagle feathers down your back...

I may exaggerate,
but why did I really *have* to employ mention of the turbine engine
to really describe the warrior's headdress? Etc. Of course the head
could have been elaborated in prose, but the psychic factor would
have been lost via a delayed delivery. Our metaphysical preference for condensation, density—has a correspondence, and
intense one, in the very elements of Indian design and ritual. I
have, by the way, an Indian dance as part 4 of Powhatan's

Daughter, the second section of the Bridge immediately following the Ave Maria which you have. I don't want to send it to you, however, until the other sections of this section are completed.

I'm glad you get the essential thing in Cutty Sark—written immediately after Ave Maria, symbolically touching not only on the sea—and its presence under the center of the bridge (this comes about midway in the poem)—but the depth and hazards of the psyche, as well—a plumb line.

The green eyes, the drums, the Rose theme, precursor of the Atlantis theme which closes the poem on the pure Mythos of time and space. In a way, the calligramme, the regatta is the "sublimation" of the "raw article" as seen personified in the bar-cafe.

Forgive my rambling. It could go on unforgivably and confusedly. I'm engrossed in a thousand problems of form and material all at once these days. One can go only so far with logic, then wilfully dream and play—and pray for the fusion.—When one's work suddenly stands up, separate and moving of itself with its own sudden life, as it must; quite separate from one's personality.

Your letter offering such kind help after the hurricane was forwarded also. You have my profoundest thanks for *all* of this. I trust you are not leaving for France until next spring; but in case it's considerably earlier be sure to let me know. I should like to have a few hours talk in NY before your departure.

> *Best wishes and sincerest affection,* —
> *Hart Crane*

Periodicals have not been forwarded yet—but I'm expecting them. I have a very faithful old lady on the other end of the line!

Winters at the time was still planning to study in France, but he was never to see Paris. After his years in Idaho, he found that his wife's health was still precarious and that she required a climate at least as dry and benign as that of northern California. He could not meet Crane in New York, and it would be another year before they met in California for a memorable four days.

Crane did receive, however, the manuscript of *The Bare Hills*, forwarded from the Isle of Pines, which he read and briefly praised.

Patterson—Nov. 21

Dear Winters:

Your ms. reached me last week. I've read it—but want further time and freedom from some work presently under my own hand before commenting. You'll understand, I'm sure.

Fundamentally it's serious and strikingly honest, and the book as a whole is organic—has unity. But more later—containing probably some "complaints."

My best to you—
Hart Crane

Within a week Crane was able to write a more detailed study of Winters's manuscript. First, he answered some queries by Winters about "Cutty Sark" and accepted his corrections of the Spanish and Latin of "Ave Maria." The manuscript that Winters sent Crane was evidently not very different from the printed version that would appear in 1927. Although a few of the poems were written in 1921, the bulk were done between 1924 and 1926. Winters was still close to them, and doubtful, and although he did not agree with Crane's preferences, which he thought stressed the rhetorical and inflated rather than the definite, he needed and was glad to have the extended commentary. At about the same time he sent the manuscript to Tate, who commented extensively. Partly from their critical stimulus, he rewrote some of the poems. But Crane did not single out any of Winters's favorites for praise, nor did Tate ("The Barnyard," "The Grosbeaks," "The Dead"). Winters prized their commentaries, and he stuck to his own motives.

Dear Winters:

Don't scratch your head further about "taeping." It's not a fish, now any manner of coitus. *Taeping* and *Ariel,* one British and the other Yankee, were noted clipper rivals in the India tea trade races of '46 or thereabouts.... And accept my hearty thanks for your corrections on the Spanish and Latin. I must have been taught Main street pig-latin to have so slighted the penultimate; however, I may possibly let this remain Elizabethanly porky, regardless. But the holy mother has already been restored to proper syllable.

I've been too harried and scrambled lately by a hundred little decisions and hesitancies incident to forms and material for the Bridge to give anything a fair reading, but I've immensely enjoyed the time spent with your poems. There isn't a bad poem in the ms., nor a weak one. Your "passion is resistant like a pane of glass," through which you filter strict pictures. Cold, sleep, stone, glass — these recurrent qualities, becoming touchstones of consciousness — are driven into the brain. They become the chainlinks of your observations and evocations. Your landscape is always solid, even when the fragility of the theme is a little tenuous, as it seems in several of the shorter, hokku-like forms.

You seem to have deliberately chosen very definite boundaries — and this certainly *helps* give your book a genuine unity.... The first stanza of *Song* (pg 34) seems to me to present possibly as accurate a definition of your particular aims as could be mustered, — your self-discipline implied in the "stiff wild hall of light." You emphasize the static element, the picture, the moment of realization, — a moveless kernel that glimmers like some mineral embedded in native rock. These: —

My very breath
Disowned

> In nights of study,
> And page by page
> I came on spring.
>
> —   —   —
>
> Dry penguins
> On the cliffs of light
>
> —   —   —
>
> Unlit windows, coffee hour by hour
> And chilling sleep—

are the kind of gleaming "facts" that hold my enthusiasm throughout your work. Such felicities, and one's exact reasons for so liking them, are hard to explain clearly. I always have to rush to metaphysics, and then I come back with tomes of complicated fragilities. I'll spare you that . . .

My favorite is "The Rows of Cold Trees." Here, as in "Eternity," "The Passing Night," "The Moonlight" and "The Crystal Sun," also—you are on "the mythical and smoky soil:" your "wave-length" deepens, the structure of thought and emotion is amplified. Here the real weight of your stones and hills comes closer, with a threat. You are more discursive—and with no loss of intensity. "José's Country," with its last line, "a fern ascending," is beautiful. Likewise "The Precincts of February" and "Resurrection."

Truly, throughout the book, you come off with all you attempt, —or seem to attempt, — "solid in the spring and serious" (I love that phrase!); a rare example in "these days of hard trying," as Marianne Moore puts it: free from affectations, stained glass effects, or nervous antics. Is the book coming out next spring? If I have developed any editorial connections by that time I should like to review it. At present—up to the present—I have never been able to persuade any editor that I could lisp in anything but numbers. A true deduction, possibly, as you may judge by this letter.

Aunt Harriet has just taken "O Carib Isle," a rather violent lyric urging the hurricane on the Isle of Pines, which, of course, *came.* I hope to get this "Quarter" etc sometime, but I'm afraid they're lost. Do write again when you have time.

With best wishes,
Hart Crane

Up to this last letter, the correspondence had been largely concerned with private matters, and except for Winters's letter from which Harriet Monroe printed a brief statement, no published statement by either man on the poetry of the other had appeared. Crane would never comment publicly on Winters (he published no reviews after 1921), but a second stage would soon be reached with Winters's enthusiastic reception and review of *White Buildings*. At the base of that review rest the letters exchanged between the two men and to a less important extent those between Winters and Tate. The last communication of 1926 is an apologetic postcard from Crane.

Patterson
[Postmarked Dec. 16, 1926]

Dear Winters — Am laid up with tonsilitis — will try to write later. Meanwhile a Merry Christmas and lucky '27.

Hart Crane

I'm wondering if my book *ever will* be out — !

The book would be out, soon, with Tate's introduction and, ultimately, Winters's review.

II

WHITE BUILDINGS

"Well a book of poems is a damned serious affair," Wallace Stevens wrote to William Carlos Williams.[1] *White Buildings* is itself a serious enough affair: the conditions surrounding its publication read like an exasperating comedy. Frustration mounted on frustration with all ending in reasonable happiness.

The first frustration came from the problem of finding a publisher willing to risk capital on a small volume of compact intense verse, and though Crane had many friends and friends of friends in the New York publishing world, he found them all writing regretful letters of rejection. Boni and Liveright, the ultimate publisher, refused the book once, then accepted it with the stipulation that Eugene O'Neill write a preface or introduction, but deciding that even the name of so distinguished a writer could not guarantee the book a market, rejected it once again. Crane's friends maintained steady pressure on Horace Liveright, however, and Allen Tate even offered to write an introduction over O'Neill's signature. Liveright eventually gave in, provided that O'Neill would write a short statement for the jacket; the introduction would be written and signed by Tate.[2]

Crane was to suffer from a common complaint of writers. Very few poets see a book in print before they are tired of it, even dismayed, having gone on to other and fresh interests. Yeats once said when asked which of his works he most liked, "*The Shadowy Waters* and the poem just completed." When *White Buildings* finally appeared, it contained no poem that had not already been printed more than six months earlier. For Crane the work "just completed" was composed of segments of *The Bridge* and the Caribbean lyrics derived from his experience on the Isle of Pines. Looking at the book put him in "an extremely distrustful mood in regard to most of [his] work."[3]

The final blow fell when on December 28, 1926, the book came from the binder. Several copies were immediately sent out for review, including the copy that Winters used, but when Allen Tate saw the book he demanded that publication be suspended, the title page changed, and the entire issue rebound. On the title page, his name was spelled "Allan Tate." Early in January Crane was troubled by the ultimate crusher of this delay:

> A detention of the book much longer is going to ruin all chance of sales from Waldo's article. Lord! is there anything else that can happen to that book! How long will it take them to put in those new title pages, I wonder.[4]

Waldo Frank's review would not appear until March; Crane need not have worried. The book received some fifteen reviews, a few of them crude in their incomprehension but most giving moderate to enthusiastic praise. Sales were another matter. Although the book was effectively sold out by April 1 of 1927, 121 of the 500 copies had been sent to reviewers and many of the copies had been remaindered. The book would not be reprinted until September of 1929.[5]

After the book, in its original form, appeared, Crane continued his letters to Winters. Like Harriet Monroe and Allen Tate and other friends and correspondents of Winters, Crane had been urged to read *The Time of Man,* one of the touchstones Winters used to determine whether people were sympathetic with his views. Winters also tried to discover whether Crane was as fascinated by boxing matches as he was. Much later in his career, Winters was to issue a mock challenge to Basil Bunting to meet him with or without gloves because of a literary offense. The challenge was obviously a joke.[6] Winters loved boxing matches and

attended university matches at Stanford and read about such figures as Tiger Flowers. In his declining years, his family bought
him a television set so that he could take his mind off his own pain
and discomfort by watching a sport that he enjoyed.

Crane's comments on Winters's *The Immobile Wind* and *The
Magpie's Shadow* are reasonable; they do lack the edge that
marks Winters's later volumes, and Crane singles out good poems
from these juvenilia. The note on *White Buildings* indicates his
natural doubts about the book and seems to ask Winters's opinions. The poem to Emily Dickinson was to be the subject of dour
comments by Winters later, but he framed the holograph copy of
it by Crane and kept in his his study.

Patterson, NY
Jan. 3, '27

Dear Winters:

Your enthusiasm prompted me to read The Time of Man. It's
a superb piece of work and I *almost* share your statement that it's
the greatest piece of narrative prose that has come out of America. It *is* in its particular *genre*. And you feel that it will stand all
kinds of tests.

I also share your interest in boxing matches. But I've seen so
few that I'm no critic. And when I come to put on the gloves myself I'm about as agile as a polar bear and wheeze like a gander. I
have heard of Tiger Flowers but never followed his career.
There's much in a name and he never should have been beaten.

The booklets from the Isle of Pines have finally reached me.
And there are several things which [I] regret are not included in
the covers of your new book. The Wizard and My Memory are
among them — and the title poem of the same booklet. Many of
the poems seem to lack the "edge" that you have in your later
work, however. This is very possibly due to a lack of confidence
which I'm sure in my own case is responsible for certain obscuri-
ties that I'm constantly accused of.

My White bldgs, now out, shocks me in some ways. I think I have grown more objective since writing some of those poems — more sympathetic with the reader. "Make my dark heavy poem light — and light" is a line from Donne which has always haunted me. But on the other hand some of Donne's greatest complexities have most delighted me. This gentleman, by the way, somehow escaped mention in Tate's introduction — but verily, I think he should have been. But I seem to have a queer mixture of tastes.

Allow me to thank you — or the Fates, if you prefer, for securing my book for review in *Poetry*. I want to read MacLeish's work as soon as possible. He is so far a complete stranger. He and Tate are now at work compiling an anthology of French and Anglo-American romantic poetry. Liveright is going to publish it, I think. I may be ill advised in mentioning this at present — so please don't advertise the project in any incidental way.

You will excuse the dull and egocentric tenor of my correspondence lately, I hope. Certain worries and tonsilities which seems to linger indefinitely make me a forbidding grouch. However, you must know how much I enjoy hearing from you — and that I hope you'll not give me up entirely. I enclose a little poem written lately to our Emily."

Best to you and your wife —

Hart Crane

Crane's mixed feelings about the publication and reception of the book remained after Winters wrote to him upon receiving his review copy on January 10. Winters's praise was unrestrained; part of that letter survives since Crane quoted it to his mother in a letter of January 23:

Yvor Winters, who is a professor of French and Spanish at the Moscow University, Idaho, writes me the following: "Your book arrived this evening, and I have read it through a couple of times. It will need many more readings, but so

far I am simply dumbfounded. Most of it is new to me, and
what I had seen is clarified by its setting. I withdraw all
minor objections I have ever made to your work. —I have
never read anything greater and have read little as great."[7]

The praise from Winters was exhilarating, especially since Crane
could vindicate his work to his family with it as evidence. Writing
to Winters he expressed a natural gratitude, and he gossipped
about the reviewing and possible British publication of *White
Buildings*. His heart was, however, still more deeply implicated in
The Bridge, and he sent Winters "The Dance" section of that
poem, at that point titled only "Powhatan's Daughter (Part IV),"
and different at very few points from the final version: six changes
in diction, eight in punctuation, none of them radical.

Patterson, NY
Jan. 19th, 1927

Dear Winters:
    Your letter of the 10th most welcomely breaks a rather long
and sober rumination I've been indulging in lately on the defects
of several of the White Buildings. . . . I'm elated that you think so
highly of the book, and if subsequent readings leave you with
even half the admiration expressed in your letter I shall be grateful to the Powers that give as well as take.
    I have been unexpectedly lucky, I think, for one whose work is
obviously so 'extreme.' Waldo Frank has written a quite vocifer-
ously friendly review which may already be out in the New Republic. Who else, besides yourself, is to review the book I don't
yet know. But two such are certainly more than compensation for
the drubbing the book is sure to get from most other hands.
Then, too, Edgell Rickword, editor of The Calendar, London, is
placing the book with a new publisher there, to whom he is acting
as advisor. However, the terms of the agreement have not been
settled yet.
    I am enclosing the Indian dance section of Powhatan's Daugh-

ter, which is a kind of fiery core to this part of the Bridge, (II). I had hoped to send you the section complete, so you would get the gradual ascent from Manhattan harbor, etc. but I'm a little too impatient to ask you a question to delay longer—and I don't know when the three antecedent sections will be finally completed. It's a minor matter, but I'm anxious to know if there is an Indian philology or symbolism concerned in the name "Maquokeeta." I chose the name at random, merely from the hearsay of a NY taxi driver who was obviously of Indian extraction (and a splendid fire-drinker by the way) who said that his Indian name was "Maquokeeta." I think he came from Missouri, or thereabouts. You know much more about Indian fable, symbolism etc. than I do. Will you let me know if the name is 'sufficient' to the role it plays in the poem? Intuitions are surprising sometimes: I didn't know at the time of writing that the serpent and eagle were such valid Indian symbols of time and space, respectively, as to have stood thus in the ritual of the Aztecs.

We are snowed in here, though it can't be as bitterly cold as it must be in northern Idaho. I find that my summer of suffocating heat and the consequently violent efforts made to adjust myself to it, have made me susceptible to all sorts of chilblains, tonsilitises and other rheumatics. I'm studying Spanish with the one dream of sometime living in Havana, Cardenas, Guadalajara, Toledo or Morocco!

> Best wishes—
> Hart Crane

P.S. —If any better name occurs to you please suggest it to me. From a purely "physical" standpoint—(sound, quantity, cadence) I'm perfectly satisfied—but it may possess some jarring connotations for all I know.

Winters settled immediately to the task of writing the review. By January 21, barely ten days after receiving the book, Winters had, on Allen Tate's advise, sent his review to Marianne Moore at

The Dial. By January 30 he thought the review was rotten, but on February 1 he was furious because Marianne Moore had returned it with a note chiding him for his enthusiasm. By February 7 he had revised the review and sent it to Harriet Monroe at *Poetry.* I cite these dates because they suggest the urgency that Winters placed on having the review in print, and as soon as possible. The original version of the review was longer than the printed one, and Winters made some strictures on "My Grandmother's Love Letters," a poem that he would later make an abortive effort to defend. Perhaps he omitted any negative comments on the poem because of Crane's letter of January 27, which arrived before the final version was settled. The only segment of *White Buildings* for which Crane claimed coherence was the "Voyages" sequence. The only poem Crane disliked and Winters singled out for comment was "North Labrador." In his copy Winters checked poems that he thought especially worthy. The check marks are naturally not dated, but it is reasonable to assume that they were made as he prepared the review: "Sunday Morning Apples," "Praise for an Urn," "In Shadow," "North Labrador," "Repose of Rivers," "Lachrymae Christi," "Recitative," "For the Marriage of Faustus and Helen," "Voyages" (no particular one is singled out).

Patterson, New York
January 27th, 1927

Dear Winters:

Your account of Pablo's sad end—that is the dialect of it—reminds me of the speech of the Cayman niggers, whom I 'visited' last summer during their annual season of mosquitoes.... I'll never forget that trip. The sixty-foot schooner had *only* 35 on it (myself the only white); the sun was practically 'equatorial' at that time and latitude; and we were becalmed—dead still—under that sun for two days (which made the whole trip 4 instead of 2) until I felt 'the very deep did rot.' But nothing stopped the enchanted tongues of those niggers.... I was marooned on the island of Grand Cayman for ten days, mostly in my room, for there wasn't an inch of screening on the island—windows down and a smudge fire going all the time. My eyes disgorged more than one smoky tear over the pages of Moby Dick—which I think saved my mind.

This sounds exaggerated, but wait until you follow the pirate's tracks! My northern blood was simply ice cream and strawberry tarts to those various families of tiny vampires—and thin it as I would, by all sorts of dieting, I was always a popular pasture. . . . Cayman, by the way, is the 'scene' of O Carib Isle, which ought to be out in Aunt Harriet's breviary and—aviary—soon.

I am certainly far from certain that you ought to feel that your surroundings, that is their lack-Easty-yeastiness, have deprived you of much. Of course there's no way of computing such matters for yourself, and how much less for another! But NY costs like hell in nerves and health. I should have been dead by this time if by a lucky hunch I hadn't written Otto Kahn a letter and secured the loan of enough money to get out awhile—over a year since, that was, and now it's about gone. I'm expecting to go back soon. And there's just as much 'metaphysics' in your landscape as mine; I know—not because I once made a flying trip to the coast and across the Canadian Rockies back—but because (and whether you like your bare hills and drunken miners or not) you've done some beautiful clean mining. That proves you enough to prove the soil too. That perfect thing, The Moonlight, is just one of a dozen other substantiations in your work. In a queer kind of way all of your book is 'growing on me.'

I suppose the sheer and enormous waste of oneself—seeing oneself go under a little deeper every day in a place like NY proposes a challenge which sometimes seems best answered by a kind of word-grenade that puzzles in most cases as much as it pleases. Or neither. But after boundless literary chatter and philandering I've come to prefer some bare hill and more solitariness than I'm strong enough to gain in the city. For approach me at any hour but the 'morning after,' and I'm all for the Mermaid again. I've worn out several kidneys and several bladders already on bootleg rum, but I seem always ready to risk another. Havana was almost a paradise to me—to have a little civilization mixed with one's

food! I am going to write a Habanera in memory of it, some-
day . . .

In most all your judgments on *White Buildings* I agree with
you. The Voyages (that is the series as a whole) I think are more
articulate than you judge them, and Grandmother's Love Letters
— while a very slight theme — seems to me to have sufficient organization to claim form.

Several I should never have included had I not felt it necessary
to fill out space. This terrible admission need not be followed, I
hope, by a darker truth as to why I felt it necessary to publish!
These include the Fernery (a fussy little Laforguian thing that I
pottered on intermittently over a longer period than anything I
ever wrote — *why* God only knows, except that Cleveland is a hell-
ish place). Then, In Shadow, a relic of my Margaret-Anderson
adolescence. Chaplinesque is fairly good as writing and as a description of the comedian of The Kid, but its mood isn't matched
to the bulk of my work, or related at all to the rest of the book. I
care little for North Labrador and Legend, and should have
omitted both had Tate not urged the contrary. Etc., etc. But I
must stop monopolizing your generous indulgence somewhere.
I'm looking forward to [a] session with you at the aforesaid Mermaid when you come east. Rum has a strange power over me, it
makes me feel quite innocent — or rather, guiltless.

Slater Brown writes me interesting news: that our 'Taeping'
was originally "T*ai*ping," and the name of some town or port in
China. I wish I had a map to tell. He finds this in a history of the
clipper 'Cutty Sark' that he's reading. This is writ by Lubbock,
too — the same who [wrote] the 'China Clippers' wherein Taeping
and Ariel keep eternal company. If I still had this book (it went
with the hurricane) I'd send it on to you. You would enjoy it
immensely. Lubbock writes only for professional mariners, no
concessions in vocabulary. And some of the anecdotes and logs
quoted are marvelous. O all the gorgeous terminology of the sea
. . . most of it gone forever now, with the sails that gave it wings.
'O the navies old and oaken/O the Temeraire no more!' sings
Melville in one of those tragic little poems he wrote those last
years when he was forgotten down on a customs wharf. . . . It was

coined all of hemp, oak, air and light. Logan Pearsall Smith pays
an interesting tribute to the sea in his book on Idiom.

Brown says that Cutty Sark means a short shirt and is also the
name for a kind of witch mentioned in Tam O'Shanter:

> When ere to drink you are inclined
> Or cutty sarks run in your mind . . . etc.

He further adds that Cutty Sark is still afloat in England where
she is being reconditioned. Hooray!

Yours, ship-shape & Bristol fash'n
Hart Crane

A Critical Interlude

The review of *White Buildings* by Winters and Allen Tate's Foreword did not make Crane's reputation, though they certainly did
it no damage.[8] Crane appreciated them both deeply, Tate's because he knew Crane and his work well and overcame memories
of a bitter personal quarrel in order to write praise only moder-
ately qualified; Winters's because he wrote only from a perception of the poetry: hence both had the merit of objectivity.

They are markedly different, and they express points of view
that distinguish their authors clearly. Tate at the time was concerned with the problem of writing poetry in a culture with no
sense of moral or symbolic agreement. Winters was interested in
poems that could be complete worlds composed of fresh perceptions. Tate admired Eliot and his accomplishment; Winters had
already reached his skepticism about *The Waste Land* and
thought that Eliot's major accomplishment was "Gerontion."
Tate's Foreword is general and speculative; Winters's review
tends toward particular discriminations. Tate used Imagism as a
pejorative term; Winters found the basis for any poetic development in the poetry that he thought of as Imagist, though his pan-
theon excluded Pound and included Dickinson and Hardy. Win-

ters did not think of Crane as in any sense an Imagist, since he saw clearly the extension of his poetry to implications that even Williams did not attain and that Winters admired and envied.

When Winters received his copy of *White Buildings* he wrote to Tate as well as to Crane and praised the Foreword, though quarreling with Tate's lofty tone toward Imagism. As far as Winters was concerned, the general could only be truly indicated by stating the concrete. The speed and density he asked from verse could only be attained in that way. At the same time he resented being compared with H. D., and he found that Crane's "Garden Abstract" was a shell of a poem, not a very good example of Imagism.

The letters Winters wrote to Tate during late January and early February of 1927, when he was writing and rewriting his review of *White Buildings,* were not those of a fellow conspirator in promoting certain poetic values. The correspondence between Tate and Winters was that of two edgy temperaments, it would eventually break off for a substantial period, and it was threatened with rupture at other times. They were seeking and following different and occasionally parallel or tangential paths, but they respected each other, as they both respected Crane.

It seems necessary to stress some of these data because even so scrupulous a scholar as Sherman Paul makes their viewpoints more single than in fact they were. A kind of historical miasma seems to be settling over the origins of modern criticism in the 1920s, so that discriminations blur and what should be gratitudes are transformed into invective. Few literary phrases have been so unfortunate as John Crowe Ransom's "The New Criticism," which some thirty-seven years after the coinage seems to have become the old orthodoxy. But at one time the work of Tate and Winters was genuinely new. Winters suffered at the hands of some of his colleagues, including one chairman who told him firmly that his publications were a disgrace to the department of English at Stanford. Burke, Winters, Tate, Blackmur, Ransom, Richards, Empson—these and others were experimenting with criticism as Pound and Eliot had with poetry—shaping innovative orders. They had the courage to see the past freshly and to affirm value not only in the past but in their contemporaries: it is one thing to take Crane seriously in the 1970s; and quite another to have had the wit and perception to have taken him seriously in 1927.

Tate certainly took Crane seriously. He saw Crane's poetry as "...the only poetry I am acquainted with which is at once contemporary and in the grand manner." He neatly dissociated him from what he took to be the limits of Imagism, the tendency toward "the dry presentation of *petites sensations*" that limited poetic vision to suggestions that could not survive at "...the direct affirmation, of a complete world."

> A series of Imagistic poems is a series of worlds. The poems of Hart Crane are facets of a single vision; they refer to a central imagination, a single evaluating power, which is at once the motive of the poetry and the form of its realization.

This brief statement sums up the problems in criticism of Crane that still persist. Winters responded to this particular passage with cheerfulness: of course a series of Imagist poems was a series of worlds. That was the strength of the method, as Winters understood it. Winters—and Crane—accepted the idea of the autonomous poem; Tate was looking for something different, a *Weltanschauung* rather than the particularly realized. Winters was to chide Tate for his obsession with the preconditions of poetry. For Winters, criticism should occur after the fact and with some modesty. Tate intended a diagnostic criticism that might lay out lines of development and borders of limitation. Hence much of his Foreword considers the relation between subject and vision in poetry since Baudelaire, using Crane as an example.

Criticism of Crane has followed the poles already designated by these two brief statements. Tate established the lineaments of criticism whether negative or positive which looks to a "central imagination, a single evaluating power, which is at once the motive of the poetry and the form of its realization." The critics following this direction see in Crane a point of view, an *optique,* which accounts for the data in an emotional and metaphorical whole. The body of his work then becomes not a set of articulated realities that are independent poems but a congeries of images and metaphors. Reading Crane then becomes reading recurrent themes and motifs that complement and enrich one another. Several wholes then can be formed from his work; these entitites are not poems but sets of emotional ambiences that can be abstracted from widely separated and disparately motivated poems. The unity resides in the critic who is not determining what happens in *The Bridge* but describing what happens in him when he reads *The Bridge.* Criticism of this type has come to dominate the field, and it is not uncommon to read books on Crane which seldom quote more than a line or two of the verse in several pages and which never quote an entire poem: the work of Crane gets assimilated into and transmuted by the sensibility of the critic, which is taken to be the sensibility of Crane himself. A great deal can be done by such procedures but the one thing that cannot be done is discrimination of poetic textures and values.

The Winters review establishes a quite different direction. The relation between subject and vision that fascinated Tate is replaced by discriminations of value in the texture and structure of the poems. An initial deference to Tate is heartfelt; Winters thought that Tate's Foreword was the best essay he had ever read on a contemporary poet. In his review he called it "thoroughly competent," and Winters implied that it had preempted ground that he would have enjoyed covering. After a brief inevitable argument against Tate's depreciation of Imagism, he turns to considering in greater detail the achievement of Crane, a poet whom he places in "the small group of contemporary masters."

His discriminations are more particularized than Tate's. In a very brief paragraph Winters describes Crane's limitations with greater cogency than anyone else has managed:

> Mr. Crane's faults appear to me to be an occasional tendency to slip into rather vague rhetoric, as in the greater part of Voyages III and IV; and an attempt to construct poems of a series of perceptions so minute and so thoroughly

insulated from each other that little unifying force or outline results, as in the case of *Possessions*.

But for Winters, Crane's faults were the least interesting part of his work. In 1927 Winters did not feel the obligation to correct poetical and critical errors or tendencies toward error which motivates much of his work from 1928 on. The review remains appreciative, stressing Crane's capacity for attaining a tone so heroic that, notably in the conclusion of *Voyages II*, it is comparable "to no one short of Marlowe." Winters admired Crane's capacity for accepting his age fully and with passion, with sensitivity adequate for exploring its complexity. He praised the "steely tangible imagery" that allowed Crane to crystallize "an infinitude of metaphysical and nervous implications." Winters recognized the capacity for concentration of power and intensity that placed Crane among "the five or six greatest poets writing in English." Winters does not list the poets, but his previous criticism suggests that he places Crane with Hardy, Robinson, Williams, and Stevens.

Winters does not use this language, but for readers of Crane, and this was certainly true for me in my youth, the verse is remarkably free of banality. It does require unremitting attention, and failure to understand seems more often an indictment of the reader than of the poet. Winters phrases that special quality of Crane's verse — and it is in English practically unique to Crane — in the clearest manner, and he even accepts the occasional obscurity as a valid strategy:

> Mr. I. A. Richards has spoken of the strategic value of obscurity, and in the case of a poet whose use of words is so subtly dense with meaning and overtone, whose poems are so free of dead but restful matter, an additional obscurity is likely to force the attention upon separate words and lines, and so facilitate at the outset an appreciation of the details as details, which may, in turn, lead to a grasp of the whole. Such has been, at any rate, the effect upon myself, who make no claim to any special oracular gifts when I say that I believe myself to have arrived at a partial understanding of this book.

Winters is not content with so lucid a general statement of the quality of Crane's work, and he goes on to cite passages that sub- stantiate his claims, having already identified what he takes to be the greatest poems: "Repose of Rivers," "For the Marriage of Faustus and Helen," "Recitative," and "Voyages II and V."

In Winters's quotation of individual lines and his stress on the individual line and word in Crane as the unit of force, he is accepting the poetics that underlay Crane's own sense of his work. Winters has not yet come to look toward harmonious total form as the way to hold all poetic elements in proportion and order; he was willing to accept the brilliant elements as ends in themselves, and in so doing he was accepting the basic modern aesthetic that underlies so much of all art since the revolutions of Cubism and Imagism. Later he was to query this supposition rigorously, and his admiration and concern for Crane's work led him to make Crane a central exhibit of certain faults that were widespread in modern verse. In early 1927 the immediate impact of Crane's verse was so powerful that he was willing to accept the freshness and surprise of Crane's language as sufficient in itself. Crane's lines

> are in themselves so dense and are fitted so closely together, they present so shining and uniform a surface, that there is no foothold, no minor charm, no condescension or assis- tance. It is extremely easy to slide off the surface without having had the slightest idea of what one has been on. I have been watching Mr. Crane's progress for about eight years, with mixed feelings of admiration, bewilderment, and jeal- ousy. My reaction to his poems has always been slow and labored; but now that I have arrived at some degree of famil- iarity with the book as a whole, I am more than ever con- vinced that he deserves the careful attention which a com- prehension of his work requires.

The review is a remarkable instance of disinterested generosity; Winters had nothing to gain from so frank and enthusiastic a comment on the verse of a man he had never met and who could not and never would do anything to help Winters's own career.

His review elicited a footnote from Harriet Monroe to the effect that no living writer merited the epithet "great," in spite of the fact that Winters was remarkably circumspect in his use of the term. Winters was convinced that Crane was a great poet and was later to insist on it in a letter to Allen Tate. But in his review he never directly called Crane a great poet, speaking of the "greatest" of Crane's poems, pointing out that the striking and unusual aspects of Crane's work were characteristic of ways in which a "great poet is almost invariably hard on pre-existing dogma, not to mention co-existing dogma." He praised Crane highly, but hardly with such excess as to deserve Monroe's tart note:

> Mr. Winters strikes the editor as somewhat over-decisive in the above review. It seems a bit hazardous, for example, to hurl the adjective *great* at any contemporary. However, the left wing, in any cause, has always flown with conviction and audacity, and it has seemed best not to attempt any clipping in this instance, but to admit an analysis of Mr. Crane's artistic motive and style as offered by a poet in complete and enthusiastic sympathy with his art.

Much later, Winters was to tax Monroe for this note, observing that she had used the epithet "great" to describe Sandburg and Millay. At this point he was content to see his review in print, and did not object to being classed with the literary left wing.

So another phase in the relations between Crane and Winters came to its close. After this point their correspondence would deal with their two ambitious poetic sequences, Winters's *Fire Sequence,* Crane's *The Bridge.* Winters had proved his usefulness and generosity, so that defeated by Marianne Moore in storming *The Dial,* he could turn his guns on Harriet Monroe at *Poetry* and win a grudging surrender.

III

EMERGING DIFFERENCES

Yvor Winters's early poetry has until recently received little attention, though it was widely published and admired from 1920 to 1928. He took leave of the style developed during that period with the publication of *The Proof* in 1930, which in its second and third sections moved toward his better known traditional manner. His *Collected Poems* of 1952 and 1960, like most volumes so titled, was a selection from his work, and in that selection only some twenty of the free verse poems were included. From 1928 until the mid-sixties, the early Winters was practically inaccessible, so that one admirer of the early work — Kenneth Rexroth — laboriously copied out the poems in libraries and then typed and bound them as a permanent part of his poetry collection. Finally, in 1966 Winters issued with an extremely interesting preface *The Early Poems of Yvor Winters, 1920-28.*[1]

The Early Poems are more numerous than the *Collected Poems*. The first volume, *The Immobile Wind,* was published in 1921, and it was undistinguished versifying in conventional manners. Little of the fierce tension of the succeeding volumes was evident and certainly none of the experimental metrics. Winters had heard of and read the major experimental writers of the period, but these juvenilia give no evidence of it. *The Magpie's Shadow* followed in the next year, written entirely in lines of six syllables, each poem limited to a single line:

Spring Rain

My doorframe smells of leaves.

The book is a collection of such bright particulars, complete in themselves and isolated.[2] It was a method that he would not follow, for in the succeeding poems in *The Bare Hills,* written except for one poem between 1921 and 1926, he uses a more complex type of poetic image and writes in that special free verse that he adapted from Williams, Stevens, and Marianne Moore. This was the Winters that Crane knew and commented on in his letters.

Winters wrote Imagist poetry, but it does not have the weaknesses that Edmund Wilson saw in other poets of the period:

> The Imagists, it seems to me, inoculated American poetry with an entirely inadequate idea of what poetry ought to be: they popularized a sort of surface poetry, poetry of description, poetry for the eye—the poetry of Amy Lowell, Mr. Sandburg and Mr. Fletcher—a poetry mainly of prose cadences and flattened prose vowels.[3]

Winters recognized these dangers, and in 1924 published an essay, "The Testament of a Stone," in which he explored the various possibilities of the poetic image.[4] With both Crane and Winters, it sometimes seems incredible that they were so young when they did the work that is now part of the basis of American literature. Winters was twenty-four when he wrote "The Testament of a Stone."

The essay is youthful, but it has the qualities of Winters's mature critical writing. It is clear and systematic; he looked on this work as an attempt to "incite the beginnings of a scientific criticism of poetry." After some preliminary notes on the nature of the poet, he makes a distinction between observation and perception, observation being casual and vague, perception being a precise differentiation between one observation and another. When two perceptions are placed together in a meaningful order, they form an image, composed of sense perception; when the observations are not of sense impressions, they can become perceptions through the intellect, and the result is the anti-image. This is as valid a perception for poetic purposes as the sensory image. Winters did not limit the elements of poetry to surfaces appealing to the eye; intellectual and moral judgment were as valid as sensory perception. Further there were sound perceptions that were expressible through the sound of words, as mental and sensory perceptions were rendered through the meaning of words. The unification of these several kinds of perceptions shaped the poem.

In Winters's sense of imagism, then, the poet was not limited, in Tate's term, to *petites sensations,* nor would a legitimate poet be satisfied with prose cadences and flattened vowels. The remainder of the essay exemplifies various categories of images and is marked by a tolerance of experimental methods that Winters would later decry.

Now that the essay has been reprinted it should take its place as the clearest justification of imagist practices. The editors of *Secession* in 1924 thought it so important that they devoted an entire issue to its publication. For Winters it stabilized his ideas and would underlie his practice. He was at that time in the midst of composing his first extensive book, *The Bare Hills.*

The hills of these poems are very bare, the hills of New Mexico, Colorado, and Idaho, sparsely settled with goatherds and miners, and equally sparse in vegetation. The time and weather are wintry, and the poet isolated. The landscape yields an occasional bird, goats, dogs, children, bees, old men, some corpses, several trees, and many rocks. The poet, although usually solitary and neglected, does have a lover at intervals, and he has an occasional ambiguous vision of God. Often the poems are charming:

April

The little goat
crops
new grass lying down

> leaps up eight inches
> into air and
> lands on four feet.
> Not a tremor —
> solid in the
> spring and serious
> he walks away.

A minor perception affectionately and engagingly presented.[5] The same kind of perception can yield a poem with greater overtone:

> Song

> Where I walk out
> to meet you on the
> cloth of burning fields

> the goldfinches
> leap up about my
> feet like angry
> dandelions

> quiver like a
> heartbeat in the
> air and are
> no more

The brevity and beauty of dandelion, goldfinch, heartbeat compose a simple memorable and poignant perception of mortality.[6]

But Winters's method did not limit him to such momentary perceptions. Both Crane and Tate admired one poem especially, and Winters retained his affection for it after the event; it was one of the few early poems published in the *Collected Poems* of 1952 and 1960.

The Row of Cold Trees

To be my own Messiah to the
burning end. Can one endure the
acrid, steeping darkness of
the brain, which glitters and is
dissipated? Night. The night is
winter and a dull man bending,
muttering above a freezing pipe;
and I, bent heavily on books; the
mountain iron in my sleep and
ringing; but the pipe has frozen, haired with
unseen veins, and cold is on the eyelids: who can
remedy this vision?

                              I have walked upon
the streets between the trees that
grew unleaved from asphalt in a night of
sweating winter in distracted silence.

                                      I have
walked among the tombs — the rushing of the air
in the rich pines above my head is that which
ceaseth not nor stirreth whence it is:
in this the sound of wind is like a flame.

It was the dumb decision of the
madness of my youth that left me with
this cold eye for the fact; that keeps me
quiet, walking toward a
stinging end: I am alone,
and, like the alligator cleaving timeless mud,
among the blessed who have Latin names.

The poem is in many ways characteristic of *The Bare Hills* in its
stoic acceptance of the human condition, its insistence on harsh

bareness, the isolation of the poet, the occasional high rhetoric, the "cold eye for the fact."[7] It is marked also by obscurity — without explanation from Winters it would be difficult to say who are the blessed who have Latin names. In fact they are the denizens of the zoological world, and the line takes off from a line in Emerson:

> Emerson's line [from the poem "Blight"] comes at the end of a passage in which he attacks the young scientists who are coming through the new cuts in the hills to study nature: "And all their botany is Latin names." My Latin name was *homo sapiens;* that of the alligator was *alligator mississippiensis.*[8]

There seems no reason for thinking of animals as blessed; at least none is given by the poem.

But the cold eye for the fact is certainly characteristic of Winters's work in *The Bare Hills,* finished by the end of 1926, and it is present in his *Fire Sequence,* which was to excite a lengthy response from Crane. Kenneth Fields points out that in the early poems

> Sometimes, owing perhaps to Winters' early interest in protozoology and biology and to certain discoveries about the nature of matter by modern physicists, the feeling comes from an intense magnification of natural events which are normally unseen, as for example in "Primavera": "Atoms seethe into/the sun..." and "the/chlorophyl booms..." The physical universe that Winters seems to be confronting in isolation, especially in the later of the experimental poems, is very close to the universe of atomic physics of the twenties as described by Whitehead and others.[9]

Crane and Tate were to be surprised and somewhat irritated by the importance that Winters placed on Jacques Loeb, a biochemist at once inventive, dogmatic and, as scientists now see it, often quite wrong in his completely mechanistic interpretation of phenomena. Winters would later write "The Invaders" as an attack on scientists; in his early years he made a distinction between the scientific technology that had wrecked the world and the scientific investigations that had altered man's knowledge of the astronomical, geological, and zoological world. Loeb, who was at the Rockefeller Institute in Chicago while Winters was growing up in the same city, was an independent and intelligent man with a deliberately reasoned sense of life that Winters found so attractive that he ascribed the qualities of *The Bare Hills* and *Fire Sequence* to Loeb. Some of Loeb's special emphases appear in the language of *Fire Sequence,* as in the closing lines:

> And in the bent heart of the seething rock
> slow crystals shiver, the fine cry of Time.

Loeb thought of the crystal as occupying an intermediate place between organic and inorganic matter.[10] More important in *Fire Sequence* is the constant turning toward and away from light and fire that parallels Loeb's obsession with heliotropism. Except for Winters and Sinclair Lewis — Loeb is the model for Gottlieb in *Arrowsmith* — the only other writer of stature who was fascinated by Loeb was Theodore Dreiser, to whom Loeb once wrote:

> It was, naturally, a gratification to me that you should take an interest in my work, which, as a rule, is not relished by the majority of literary people on account of the frankly materialistic or chemical conception of life expressed in my writings. It would give me great pleasure to meet you personally, since I have followed your literary career with special interest. Needless to say, I am not a romanticist in literature.[11]

Among Loeb's many books, the most general and typical is *The Mechanistic Conception of Life.*

This, then, is some of the background of the succeeding letters from Crane to Winters. Those letters exhibit the consequences of an intellectual debate involving Tate as well as Crane and Winters. Tate was absorbed in a metaphysical quest that started from the same horror that affected Winters, a horror of solipsism.[12] Winters had little interest in Tate's absorption with the metaphysical problem; his interests were and would remain primarily ethical. He was at that time willing to accept the scientific view and did not think of it as incompatible with poetry. If poetry could not live with critical intelligence, then so much the worse for poetry. But he saw no reason why poetry could not live with the intelligence and every reason why it should. His extensive readings and studies in the sciences convinced him that the ethical and emotional consequences of modern science were greater than any impact that metaphysical speculation had had for centuries. Alas, as Winters would later admit, he then knew very little of the history and practice of philosophy.[13] What he did see in the sciences were practical and emotional consequences. He was amused when Tate wrote to him that the "forces" spoken of in physics were "abstractions" and wryly observed that Tate himself was a force. Science was concrete and definite, as he wanted poetry to be, while metaphysical systems tended to be mutually translatable and mushy. Tate's desire for a complete explanation of the cosmos did not interest him and seemed poetically irrelevant; after all, poetry dealt with men.

Winters was always something of a systematic taxonomist of literature, and he was an intellectual skeptic, a fact that evades many of his critics. He believed in an orderly universe and could not accept the idea that art imposed order on chaos, but he was by no means certain that man could perceive the total order of the cosmos. In fact he was repelled by that concept and adduced Hardy, Joyce, and Synge as examples of great writers who had no complete explanation of the universe. Although the point of view that I here ascribe to Winters is abstracted from his letters to Allen Tate in early 1927, it is surely the same attitude articulated in the lost letters to Crane, to which Crane reacted with some acerbity. Crane would have been mollified if he had known that

Winters did not see Crane's work as depending on a metaphysic any more than Chaucer's depended on astrology. Winters saw *The Bridge* as a clinching argument on his behalf against Tate's view that it was impossible to write great poetry in the modern world. To Winters, the poet's job was precisely to embody the greatness of art and thus refute all a priori theories. What mattered, finally, was the beauty of art and the desirability of being an artist. Art would be imperfect—even in so great a work as *The Bridge* there were elements of decadence—but all would be well for the writer who knew his medium, his intentions, and his material, so long as he believed that the result (the poem) was necessary to life.

Art was based on direct full perception of experience; criticism on direct full perception of works of art. From that point of view metaphysical speculation on the impossibility of perception with meaning was whimsy and moonshine. Winters would, as most readers of his later work know, come to stress the importance of the intelligence to what seems the detriment of perception, but what he really wanted was a fuller perception, using "perception" in a sense somewhat close to Merleau-Ponty's.

But Winters was not occupied only with these large speculations. He was working on the *Fire Sequence,* and he was writing long critiques of Tate's poems and flooding Tate—and Crane—with letters. Between January 30 and February 1 of 1927, he sent Tate four letters totalling three thousand words, about fifteen hundred words of commentary on a group of Tate's poems and, in addition, several of his own poems. Tate was naturally overwhelmed by this energetic interest, but he replied[14] almost immediately (February 5):

Dear Winters:

Please struggle through my script (which is unreadable); my typewriter is jammed this morning.

First, your damn fine, intelligent, and complete evisceration of my poems. It is the only thorough criticism I've ever had—I don't mean the only attack—and I find it very hard to disagree with it in the main. I think, however, your analysis point by point largely extends the more abstract principles which you advance in the general discussions we've been having. Through this I see an escape. At the same time, there is no escape from your dislike, from your sense of the imperfections of my work. Your attack is not something to be angry at; it is not pretentiously stupid; it is very acute. It is something to understand. I invariably make an effort to understand what I respect, however upsetting it may be.

The heart of your criticism is of course its purest phase. It refers to the simple exercise of craft common to all poets of whatever tendency. Much of my work, as you say, is unfinished, rough, unrealized. Yet this deficiency—which I do not deny—is not due to laziness or lack of unrest about my work. (I am lazy in other respects, but that's something else entirely). I think there is a particular stage in the creative process—or, rather, one quality of it which runs all through it which I have not yet succeeded in mastering. It is the complete control of the power of sustaining the central vision of the poem from beginning to end. Nevertheless, here is the loophole through which I see my best defense against your criticism and, also, a further confirmation of my idea of the theme-vision relation.

I shouldn't stand by the description of you as a "lyric" poet to the end, but you are one in so far as the form of the poem proceeds internally from you and is not conditioned by the demands of some external purpose. For instance, Milton, oppositely, was always conditioned by the letter of the Bible. . . . I think, as you are disposed to think, that I possess considerable power as a poet, but I have never exhibited it completely. I think the failure is due to my lack of something to write *about,* ready to hand. My mind doesn't extend forms into its outer world; but it can assimilate a given world. If you answer that a person in this state is *a priori* not a poet, I shall have to reply, Winters, you're a damn fool. . . . I can't sustain a vision from within, but I can articulate one from without. I think this accounts for the mixture of qualities which you find, for example, in The Idiot.

You observe that I repeat the *about* in connection with poetry; I do it in face of your second letter of Jan. 30th. I can still retain it and accept in entirety your distinction, What-is-done *vs* What-is-done-to-something. In fact, I have written a long essay arguing that very point. I suggest that we suspend this part of the diatribe until I can show you this essay (which is very learned and professorial); it will be out in a week or ten days. For the time being, I can only assert that while the critical problem *par excellence* is What-is-done, the backward extensions of the critical problem lead to an analysis of the types of experience to which something may be done at a given time. In 1400 the scholastic philosophy, with all its machinery, was a definite object of poetic experience; it is that no longer. You will have to agree that the critical problem is concerned with this aspect of poetry. It is only when some blind Hegelian moralist asserts that a *particular* subject-matter is exclusively poetic that my trouble begins. My doctrine is simply that the most universal poetry, the most comprehensive, occurs in an age of great objective schemes of thought. I don't give a damn for any special scheme; I care only for the poetry which is made possible by it. In short, as a critic I am concerned with the possibility of major poetry. I think a major poem can be as brief as eight, five, or nine lines; it can exceed 2,000 or 20,000.

This gets pretty far away from my poems, and the inference which you are drawing is doubtless just.

In detail, your criticism is devilishly accurate. But I think your undeveloped nerve-center exposes its atrophy in the comment on the *Sonnet to Beauty*. "The unhappy error we bewail" is not intrinsically bad; no phrase is; and I think it has a quality here which your taste cuts you off from. But there's no argument at this point; there is a stone wall: we are shouting over it. We communicate but we do not see.

The remainder of this letter responds to Winters's request that Tate join him in a protest against *The Dial*, arising in part from Marianne Moore's refusal to print Winters's review of *White*

Buildings. And once again, *The Time of Man* enters: "F. M. Ford has just lent me *The Time of Man.* He says it's great." The letter concludes with a statement that seems prophetic of later critiques of Winters:

You know, I believe if you lived in the East the extremely inter-esting acrimony of your letters would soften. I don't see the East as a softener of ire. Isolation is bad for the temper. Please forgive me—but I have gone through it myself, and I didn't bear it so beautifully, so productively, as you do.

Yours,

Tate

This was advice that Winters could not take, partly because of family health problems but also because Winters came genuinely to love the benign climate, the good cheap wine of Northern Cali-fornia and the pastoral life that he and Janet Lewis would con-struct in Palo Alto with a good academic atmosphere part of their immediate ambience. Whatever his troubles at Stanford, they were not the troubles of complete isolation in a harsh climate and a genuinely provincial university.

Within a few days of the compelling and complimentary letter from Tate, Winters received a brief handwritten note from Crane, once again in the throes of job-seeking and angered, as Tate and Winters were, by Marianne Moore's rejection of the re-view of *White Buildings.* He had received from Winters several of his translations—Winters was then translating from French, Spanish, Portuguese, German, and Latin—and complimentary remarks on the "Dance" section of *The Bridge.* Of his numerous translations, Winters certainly sent his version of the famous Spanish ballad "Fontefrida," though he was also pleased with his work on du Bellay, Mallarmé, Verlaine, and Baudelaire. Isolated Winters was, which accounts for the almost frantic output of letters, but as Tate remarked, he was bearing the isolation productively. With his heavy teaching load and his constant drive toward perfection (and recognition), Winters had reason for needing some rest.

Provincetown Playhouse
133 Macdougal Street, New York

Feb. 9 '27

Dear Winters:

I'm in the usual crazy state of mind incident to looking for a job. Thanks for your splendid letters which have been forwarded to me from Patterson. If I don't find something by the end of this week I'm going back to the woods again. That is the place to address me until I say other wise anyway. (Though I don't deserve more until I can write *you* again)....

Tate was about as peeved as you about the Moore rejection. And of course I'm damned sorry myself. Well—we all will just have to *wait* I guess. We may get a magazine in this USA sometime. The translation I'm very glad to have—though I can't read anything in the present rush. The Fire Sequence hasn't come yet.

Hope you are soon feeling better & more rested.

Faithfully yours—
Hart Crane

Your opinion of the Indian Dance makes me very happy.

Winters then sent Tate some notes on "Dynamism" that occasioned considerable conflict between him and Tate. Tate showed the notes to Crane, at Winters's request, and Crane joined the argument briefly in this letter but to greater extent when he had the leisure. Under pressure from Tate and Crane, Winters would qualify his argument.

Patterson
February 23 '27

Dear Winters:

Tate just sent up the enclosed Notes of yours, which I have enjoyed reading a great deal. I think you are right, in general, and where I fail to agree with you I think Tate hits the weak links pretty well. I go even further in disagreement with your finale, however, and venture to suggest that your scientific viewpoint is pretty much hugger-mugger. It may serve its purpose, however, in stimulating you—personally—but I can't see where it has any absolute value. No such incantation can lay life bare, or bring it a bit nearer—for me. But I desist from further comments right now: I'm beset with too many urgencies and quandaries to have a very good head. I'm postponing comment on the Fire Sequence also, which I've read—and like even better than the Bare Hills.

All best to you,
Hart Crane

The argument about metaphysics and science would continue. Winters sent some further notes to Crane to share with Tate. But for Crane the chief matter at hand was not the theoretical excursuses but the *Fire Sequence:*

Patterson
Thursday Feb 24

Dear Allen:

I wish I could keep up with Winters. I already owe him several letters, besides comment on the ms. of his "Fire Sequence," which awaited me when I returned from town. All his work is so genuine that it takes close attention, meditation and blood and bone to answer. . . . At present it's too much for me, so I've sent the manifesto on with a brief note to the effect that I agree with most of

your marginalia, i.e., where I differ with him. Though I go further than you do in qualification of the Loeb-physics-etc. recipe.
. . . Pure hocus-pocus for the poet. Just one out [of] a five-thou-
sand other scientific similes, equally good to go by (regardless of
their veracity) — and I venture to say that Winters' work suffers
already from such arbitrary torturings — all for the sake of a neat
little point of reference. What good will it do him to go on repeat-
ing in the background of every poem that "life is some slight dis-
turbance of the balance," etc., etc?! But we all must have some
kind of incantation, I suppose. Though I'd rather adopt some of
Blake's aphorisms. They're abstract enough. And a lot truer than
the latest combination of scientific terms.

Crane was right in his intuition that Winters would not be happy
about his preference for "Bison" — Winters excised it from the sequence and it appears in none of the printed versions, though he
did publish it later in *The Proof*. It is impossible to follow completely Crane's observations because he had before him a typescript that included poems ultimately dropped, so that the num-
bering of the poems is not that of the printed versions.[15]

Patterson, NY
February 26th, '27

Dear Winters:
    I can't say exactly why, but I have the suspicion that you will
somehow be disappointed in my judgment for liking *Bison* the
best of any poem in the Sequence. And I think that *November*
and *Snow-Ghost* both fall in the same superlative class. In each of
these your theme and emotion develop without break — to the
end. Of course I'm not giving much consideration to your Loeb-
biochemic theories, and it may be that you succeed in certain
other of the poems much better — in that regard. But I like such
things as the marvelous suggestion of purity in Snow-Ghost, like
the dissection of a veritable nerve-fibre,

'invisible save on this plane of light'

and the sustained assault and vibration of November. Bison is one of those things beyond analytic appreciation, like your Moonlight.

At times you betray a kind of moral zeal—a preoccupation with the gauntness and bareness of things which sometimes gets in my way in trying to discover the particular properties of certain poems. It is so evident as to be distracting at times, and I cannot help feeling it to be a fault—at least it hinders the reader from accepting your poem on its pure aesthetic merits—and isolates or tends to isolate the poem from a spontaneous reception into the reader's sensibility. But since reading your Manifesto I'm better prepared to reckon your intentions, perhaps. Laying Life bare is all very well, but I think the Lady is best approached with a less obvious or deliberate signal than an upraised ax, if you get what I mean. It might be better in some cases to swim around with her a little while. For I feel a kind of vertical strain in some of your poems; and I am either not keen enough to follow you as far below the surface as you go, or else you don't penetrate the surface as readily always as you imagine you do.

Thus, out of *Coal* I get little more than an expository statement of what is later evident as your main intention in the succeeding poems. That makes it the best poem for the start of the book. No. 2 is a good "humanization' of the same theme—'your thighs that seethe interminably'—a beautiful dynamic metaphor. No. 3 is a sharp, clean watercolor. Nos. 4, 5 & 6 puzzle me. As impressions they continue like 3—to relate man to the landscape, the idiom is forceful—but I feel myself missing many of the connotations or implications beyond that. I get more from 7, *A Miner,* than from the sum of the other three, despite their brilliant counterpoint.

It seems to me that your general practice (and it is true likewise of nearly all imagists) has been too exclusive a concentration on the epithet—and the cost of the verb-dynamics of the poem as a whole. And consequently at the expense of the organic movement of the poem. Your poems never fall apart in the sense that one portion is out of key or focus with another, but they sometimes

seem to lack the kind of progression which gives them the necessary conviction—the necessary completion or 'overtone' identifying them or their details with what I must call for lack of a better
term—universal experience. I feel some of them to be too arbitrarily directed, if anything—too 'pure'—sometimes as isolated as
a chemical experiment. The intellect is capable of emotional fire,
but far from all its 'moods' seem to me emotionally adaptable to
the creation of poetry. At least that's my feeling about your 'cold
eye for the fact,' though, paradoxically it would be hard for me to
find two poems which better express the pure functioning of the
intellect (and the beauty of such) than the very poem where that
'eye' is mentioned, and the aforepraised *Snow-Ghost*. But that is
because you got 'emotional' about your intellect and allowed your
experience more imaginative range than you sometimes do when
bent on objectifying something outside yourself.

No. 8 I like—as a keen drawing. No. 9 seems to me again too
'chemical,' also 10, excepting 'the globe of winter.' 11 is too
obscure, to me; 12 seems strained. 14 moves—and is beautiful,
and the next two are certainly fine. The painter-poem begins a
little like one of Cummings'—'To Picasso'—but resemblances
stop at once. *The Orange Tree* is the perfect type of imagist
poem, even to the 'classic leaf' which it convincingly bears. *Los
Angeles* and *Idaho* achieve a perfect contrast. *The Bitter Moon*
and *December Sunset* get lost in abstractions that don't carry over
—at least to me. The beautiful rhythm of *The Deep*, despite several fine lines, leaves me 'cold,' indeed, as may be intended.

But this Sequence has a unity which your Bare Hills did not
have—at least to the same solid degree. I envy you your method
on one hand, and decry you for it on another. For I feel you are
very consciously limiting yourself at times, and much more so
than I should care to do. Not that I haven't a 'method'—but that
our methods differ more than at first I thought they did. You
want to strike directly inward, whereas I never consciously pre-
meditate striking at all; I am interested mainly in a *construction*,
autonomous,—the validity of whose abstract 'life' of course, is de-
pendent on organic correspondences to Nature. In this sense

White Bldgs has two symbolic meanings, or connotations, its primary one being metaphysic-mechanical: it is only secondarily 'Woolworthian.'

For such as the above reasons you will probably forgive me for feeling my method as inherently much more 'dynamic' than Williams'—though it would take a lot of space to qualify this. I do not think that your method—as I understand it—is any less dynamic than mine. (Your manifesto has started me on all this.) I merely question the fertility of your key-symbol for it, the Loeb doctrine,—your (to me) superstitious conviction that Science strips Nature bare, and all that. Science may not decorate nature the way a minor poet does, but it nevertheless substitutes just one costume (set of terms) after another, one more split hair after another falls on Nature's bosom—the ultimate truth of any of which has been as well expressed by poetry—long since. Blake expressed the concept of Relativity long before science invented the term. Science is awfully stimulating—and should be used, but since it has become, as lately, an actual emotion, I think it is dangerous when uncontrolled. To me it must always remain an implement, not an oracle.

Living expansively enough in the current of the times—one becomes sufficiently infected, I suppose, to faithfully represent in one's reactions the characteristics of the period. If one is an artist the harmonious organization of such prejudices, aptitudes, etc.— sub speciae aeternitatis—tends to determine the cultural history of the age. But I think one has to turn away from the age at times —as much as possible—in order to see it at all intensely or synthetically. For as our vision of 'eternity' is itself a product of the age we live in—it can't very well be overlooked. At least I must conceive all or most of my poems under this process, regardless of whether or not they 'fit' the time. I *must*, perforce, use the materials of the time, or the terms of my material will lack edge,— reality; one doesn't have to feel any great enthusiasm for one's age before utilizing the immediate materials it proffers. Personally— I think that these materials contain enough direction—enough dynamism in themselves—to eradicate the question or the primal importance of the question—as to just *where* they are taking us. Our intuitive selection of these materials on the basis of their appeal to us (their power) will ultimately determine our 'position' in time, historically speaking. We can't but be intuitive—our logic, the logic we choose to balance our 'intuitions' is intuitively selected. I must always write from the standpoint of Adam,—or rather, I must always fool myself that Adam 'felt the same way about it.' And you have granted me the feat at least of digesting machinery as successfully as nightingales!

There are other things that your manifesto prompts me to question, but I must break off this wild nonsense somewhere.... I've felt quite guilty for having put you (and others) to such lengthy pains anent the investigation of Maquokeeta. I feel perfectly reassured, however, for obviously the name isn't some notorious joke. Even if it has no existence as a name it's quite practical for my purposes, as it certainly *sounds* Indian enough to apply to a redskin. Thanks for forwarding the Cartwright notice.

I haven't yet had time to study the translations the way I want to. Your scholarship simply amazes me. I find several of the poems in a little anthology I have—Las Cien Mejores Poesías—, but I make slow progress in any language. But the pure sensuous appeal of Spanish is—almost—enough to induce me to struggle with it. They may be a messy lot, as you say—but their architecture, customs and general 'air' please me immensely—from the little I've seen. We all have some such personal and inexplicable impulses.

Please pardon this long harangue—and let me hear from you soon. Is the Bare Hills out yet?

All best to you and Janet Lewis,
Hart Crane

This is one of the most important letters that Crane wrote to Winters. It shows that while Winters's appreciation of Crane and especially of the bulk of *The Bridge* remained steady, the two men were on very different tracks. Four of the poems that Crane singled out for praise and comment were excised from the final version of the *Fire Sequence* and printed later in *The Proof;* three of the poems were never printed by Winters in any form. Crane was skeptical of Winters's bias toward the scientific view and could not appreciate the seriousness of Winters's desire to "lay life bare." The phrase is not Crane's invention; it was used by Winters on other occasions and is evidently a quotation from the two manifestos he sent to Crane and Tate. But perhaps more important in the divergences that were to grow are the closing segments of the letter where Crane defends the intuitive following of the power of the age as proper to poetry; this stress on intuition and the power of the age were to be increasingly a cause of distress to Winters. He was further annoyed by what he told Tate was Crane's lecture on the dangers of imagism.

Crane was, however, an extremely astute critic of the *Fire Sequence* and of Winters's motives. Especially after the poems mentioned by Crane were excised, this sequence is preoccupied with "the gauntness and bareness of things" to an unrelieved extent. There is a "vertical strain" in some of the poems that is puzzling and even obscure, so that like Crane I often have difficulty in determining whether I am missing something or the poem is. The poems do lack "overtone" and the poems that Crane identifies as 4, 5, and 6 (almost surely the poems so numbered in both printed versions, "Bill," "The Vanquished," and "The Victor") while interesting do not seem to move the sequence forward and are in fact summed up by the following poem ("A Miner") so thoroughly that if surgery were necessary those poems would seem reasonable candidates. Crane's comments that Winters seemed to be "very consciously limiting" himself at times express some of the discomfort that I feel with much of the sequence. And Crane strikes a central chord when he points out that many of the better moments in these poems occur when Winters's emotionality about the intellect compels him to a greater imaginative range.

Winters himself came to be discontented with the *Fire Sequence*. By June of 1927 he saw only three of the poems—"Liberation," "November," "The Bitter Moon"—as providing seeds for his continuing work. Winters was every bit as hard on his own work as he ever was on any other poet's, and the *Fire Sequence* was in important ways a turning point in his writing. The results would not immediately appear, but he was coming to an ending. Crane's criticism chimed with something in Winters's own state of mind, more important than Crane's chiding him for his scientific interests, and at least temporarily more important than Crane's affirming the importance of living in "the current of the times" and his relative indifference to where that current might be taking poets. On receiving Crane's comments, Winters sent the *Fire Sequence* to Tate, noting dourly Crane's objection to excessive abstraction in "The Bitter Moon" after writing several pages on the evils of imagism. Winters took Crane's comments seriously; he consulted another poet.

The freedom and frankness of the correspondence was such that Crane did not expect Winters to be seriously annoyed by his rather severe strictures on Winters's basic point of view, so that shortly after his long letter he sent Winters a segment of *The Bridge,* the "Three Songs" of section five:

Patterson, NY
March 6th, '27

Dear Winters:

More and more . . . ! This is old stuff of last summer's. It may not be especially interesting but it belongs in my original plan of the Bridge, following directly on Cutty Sark. I've been holding it back more-or-less because I'm not doing any writing lately — can't, for a number of worrisome reasons, — and have rather enjoyed "pottering" over such sections as have seemed to lack a final sense of conviction. As I'm afraid I can't do the enclosed any more service you may as well bear the brunt of my egoism — and receive them as generously as you think their merits may deserve.

The two final sections, The Tunnel (the hell of the subway) and Atlantis may never be finally satisfactory, but I may send them on to you sometime soon. However, don't infer that I expect immediate answers or comment on any of this copious quotation; you have been favulously generous already!

best wishes,
Hart Crane

Winters had responded to Crane's letter on the *Fire Sequence* and related matters in such terms that Crane saw little difference between their basic points of view, at least theoretically.

Patterson
March 12

Dear Winters:

My eyes have gone bad—conjunctivitis—and I can't see to read much for the present. Just want to thank you for the Spanish libros which came last week. It looks like a fine bunch and will keep me busy for a long time. Pardon my brevity . . .

Yrs—
Hart Crane

Your letter of Mar. 2nd gave me a better perspective of your ideas. . . . Not that it's necessary—but our theoretical differences seem to [be]—almost negligibly minor.

The *Fire Sequence* was published in *American Caravan* for 1927, at least those parts of it that Winters accepted as tolerable. For the next two years he tried to shape around it a book of poems, integrating it with new works, restoring sections that had been abandoned. It never would form the center of a major statement that Winters hoped for, and eventually Winters salvaged for book publication only two of the seventeen poems in *Ameri-*

can Caravan, at least until the *Early Poems* appeared. When seeking reasons for Winters's change in point of view and poetic method after 1928, his ultimate dissatisfaction with the *Fire Sequence,* his sense of it as a poetic and public failure should take a primary place. Seeking intensity of vision, he created a certain tightness and constriction. The bareness and gauntness that Crane saw made for a poetry harsh but not moving. Winters had come to an impasse. Although he continued writing in free verse and he would always hold to the concepts of the image that appeared in "The Testament of a Stone," he was ready for an infusion of fresh means, and with that an extended and altered point of view. This would not develop at once and thoroughly but slowly over the years, involving a total reassesment of the poetics that he had earned through the studies and affections of his youth. His genuine doubts about the *Fire Sequence,* his sense that it did not grant currency to his true motives and possibilities, were in effect a test both personal and poetic. He found some of his difficulties shared by Crane and Tate in different manners, Crane with his low productivity because of family matters and other personal troubles, Tate partly paralyzed by his sense that the modern world simply did not provide an arena for important poetry. The period immediately following the *Fire Sequence* was one of doubt and self-query.

IV

PROGRESS ON *THE BRIDGE*

In the Crane-Winters papers there are two versions of *The Bridge,* the first typescript version including all the poem except for the three sections completed in 1929 ("Indiana," "Cape Hatteras," and "Quaker Hill"). When the entire poem was finished, Crane sent Winters a carbon of the version that would be published by Black Sun Press and Liveright; it is essentially the familiar final text. At some point, probably during early 1927, Crane sent Winters a tentative table of contents for the poem. (See following page.) In this plan, the ultimate order of "Cape Hatteras" and "Cutty Sark" is reversed, "The Mango Tree" is tentatively included, two sections never written are listed, "The Calgary Express" and "1920 Whistles"; and "Quaker Hill" is not mentioned. The conception of the poem was in a state of flux, and it would remain so. Schwartz and Schweik note that

> Crane had originally planned additional sections of *The Bridge,* but they were never completed and probably never started: "The Cyder Cask," "The Calgary Express," a Negro Pullman porter's version of the John Brown legend, and a New Year's Eve fantasy called "1927 Whistles."[1]

But on August 12, 1926, Crane wrote to Waldo Frank that "Even the subway and 'Calgary Express' are largely finished."[2] My own suspicion is that what Crane at first thought of as "Calgary

Projected plan of THE BRIDGE

\# Dedication -to Brooklyn Bridge

\#1 -Ave Maria

  2 -Powhatan's Daughter (
  \# (1) The Harbor Dawn
  \# (2) Van Winkle
    (3) The River
  \# (4) The Dance
    (5) Indiana

  3 -Cape Hatteras

\# 4 -Cutty Sark

\# 5 -The Mango Tree   — *may not use this*

\# 6 -Three Songs

  7 -The Calgary Express

  8 -1920 Whistles   —— *ditto*

\# 9 -The Tunnel

\# 10 -Atlantis

Those marked # are completed.

Express" was assimilated into the final version of "The River."

By early 1927 Winters had seen several segments of *The Bridge*, though not all those that were completed; Crane withheld "The Tunnel" and "Atlantis" and sent them later in the year. Now that the business of *White Buildings* had come to its conclusion and Crane had made his comments on the *Fire Sequence*, he returned to his current work. Although he published more individual poems than in any year of his life, 1927 was not a productive year for Crane. Most of them had been written during his great creative period in the preceding year at the Isle of Pines. For a poet who labored with such intensity as Crane, seeing nineteen poems appear in print in a single year was a great accomplishment. At the same time, his powers were going into that decline which marred and embittered his last years.

His family troubles increased. His mother went through her second divorce, and his father's adored second wife died slowly and painfully of cancer. The only compensation in this suffering came from the fact that it drew father and son together. Crane's grandmother slipped into ill health and became practically helpless. His mother grew more and more distressed.

His letters to Winters brush these matters only lightly. He is interested in their differences in taste, grateful for those differences in experience and theory which allow them to see each other's work freshly and helpfully. The correspondence kept poetry at the direct center of attention; that may, considering the state of Crane's life, have been its reward.

He could write to Winters about his problems with *The Bridge*, the six years that lay behind its current state, and the further six years that might precede its completion. Crane's poetic problems are very clearly expressed in this letter, his dependence on intuition and revelation, his need for something more than ordinary mental logic.

On the same day as Crane's letter, Winters was writing to Tate about the grandeur of *The Bridge* and the greatness of the lizard passage in "The Dance." The novelty and freshness and scale of conception led Winters to believe that when completed the poem would be as great as anything by Marlowe. Part of the evidence

he was considering was the "Three Songs," sent to him recently by
Crane, with an epigraph from Marlowe's *Hero and Leander*.

Patterson, NY
19 March '27

Dear Winters:

It's reassuring to know that you care for the Three Songs.
Doubts, accidentally or justifiably, accumulate sometimes
around certain pieces of work that never touch others. Sometimes
they are based on the fear that the material or viewpoint featured
is too personal to the writer, or again it may be the question of
technique employed — questions of pure form. No amount of rag-
ging would ever have convinced me, for instance, that Ave Maria
wasn't primarily solid and valid, and I could say the same of the
Indian dance and certain other poems. I hope that you don't
mind my rather impertinent practice of 'trying out' so many
things on you! In this respect I consider that our differences of
'experience' and our differences on theoretical matters are all to
the good. I only regret that my ideas, as such, are so relatively
incoherent — especially now, owing to a thousand quandaries in
grappling with resistant materials — that I'm not able to offer
more interesting or pertinent comment on the things you've been
sending me.

It's impossible to imagine without undertaking a like problem
oneself — what endless problems arise in carrying forward the conception of a theme like the Bridge. It takes more than ordinary
mental logic, of course, to fuse all the multitudinous aspects of
such a theme — I carried the embryonic Idea of the poem about
with me for six years before I ever wrote a line. Then there was a
sudden impetus, the results of which you have seen almost entirely. I am beginning to think that it may be six more years before the materials for the rest of the poem shall have reached a
sufficiently mature organization to be ready for paper. Logic or
no logic, I can never do anything that is worth while without the
assent of my intuitions. The logical progression of the Bridge is

well in my mind. But one has to even fight that! At least one has
to be ready to doubt its validity thoroughly on the slightest whis-
pering approach of what I might call 'temperature' — the condition for organic fusion of experience, logical or no. Melville
didn't write good verse, but the following lines at least show him
to have realized the nature of the problem:

> In placid hours well pleased we dream
> Of many a brave, unbodied dream;
> But form to lend, pulsed life create,
> What unlike things must meet and mate;
> A flame to meet, a mind to freeze;
> Sad patience, joyous energies;
> Humility, yet pride and scorn;
> Instinct and study; love and hate;
> Audacity, reverence. These must mate
> And fuse with Jacob's mystic heart,
> To wrestle with the angel — Art.

This is not quoted for your edification or information. It gives
you or at least is so intended — nothing more than the primitive
attitude I take toward both materials and aesthetic dogmas.
There seems to me really no convincing modus operandi but what
you might call alert blindness. Aesthetic speculations, etc. are of
course endlessly interesting to me and stimulating. But not one
that I have ever encountered has been quite equal to the necessary assimilation of experience — the artist's chief problem. I
admit many biases. For instance, that I have a more or less religious attitude toward creation and expression. I respond more to
revelation — or what seems revelation to me — than I do to what
seems to me 'repetitious' — however classic and noble. That is one
reason why Williams probably means less to me than to you. I
wish we could have a conversation on the subject of Williams —
one is so at a disadvantage in writing out paragraphs which a
monosyllable would settle in conversation.

There is no doubt of the charm of almost all of W's work. I
except the Paterson and Struggle of Wings lately published in the
Dial. I think them both highly disorganized. But in most of Wil-

liams' work I feel the kind of observations and emotions being 'made' which seem to me too casual, however delightfully phrased, to be especially interesting. I feel much the same about most of Whitman. But with Whitman there is a steady current — under or overtone — that scarcely ever forsakes him. And a rhythm that almost constantly bespeaks the ineffable 'word' that he has to speak. This 'tone,' assertion, or whatever — emerges through all the paradoxes and contradictions in his work. It doesn't try to be logical. It is an operation of some universal law which he apprehends but which cannot be expressed in any one attitude or formula. One either grasps it or one doesn't. When it comes out in a thing like the first 'paragraph' of Out of the Cradle Endlessly Rocking it is overwhelming. The man is both distant and near:

> This is the far-off depth and height reflecting
>   my own face;
> This is the thoughtful merge of myself, and the
>   outlet again.

Williams writes poems to the household gods — and you get a picture of a delightful man bent on appreciating the best that is given to him — sometimes, too often — dramatizing trifles in the classic manner of the old Chinese poets, and occasionally giving a metaphysical twist to his experience which is truly marvelous. To my mind he has written at least a dozen superb poems: Postlude, To Mark Antony in Heaven, A Goodnight, The Hunter, — these are my favorites added to some things in Spring & All which I haven't had with me since the hurricane. I see nothing whatever Shakespearian about him however — unless you mean that he is in attitude not overweeningly romantic. You mistake me if you think that I value non-representative art more than representative. That isn't at all what I meant by my little recipe. It must be both, of course — I mean a poem or a picture must have its own legs — no matter what it's carrying. But it must convey and even accentuate the reality of its subject. That's the service of metaphor. And it must not only convey but locate and focus the *value* of the material in our complete consciousness. W's goes far this way in many poems — in others he seems to me to go off the track as badly as I often do, to judge by some of the strange interpretations I get of some of my poems. Personally I often delight in some of these excursions of W's — but I don't 'approve' of them. They are too precious, insulate to all but — at least I fancy — a few 'choice spirits' and even then rather toylike. I don't mean that I'm a democrat. But I don't believe in encouraging the fancy — as long as there is imagination. To me, The Rose is Obsolete, represents this phase of W's.

I must stop rambling — if for no other reason than that the RFD is approaching. Have you really read much of Cummings' poetry? I suspect you haven't — else you would have more to say for him. Have you read his privately printed book called *&* — or the *IS5* (Boni & Liveright) which contains some of the best in the former — ? Tulips and Chimneys contains some of his worst sentimentalities. But the sensibility of the man is equal to Donne's — and if he had only cared to take a little more pains and organize — he'd be superb. I wish you'd let me know if you haven't read *&*. I'd like to make you a few copies of my favorites if you haven't.

I wish you would maintain a better opinion of your Sequence. It deserves it. You haven't quite the range of Williams — at least I don't quite think you have — but you're much more essentialized and certainly as adept. At any rate — I don't believe in impeccability — hang it all, let yourself go more, regardless of poetics.

> *Best wishes—*
> *Hart Crane*

I've ordered the Indian record finally, after a hell of a time perusing catalogues. I had begun to think you had misnamed it.
I see you're in the forthcoming transition. Do they pay anything? Marianne has finally taken something: P's Daughter's Dance.

Crane was asking the impossible. Even at this early stage in his career, Winters was obsessed with the relation between theory and practice, practice implicit in theory, theory implicit in practice. His early essays, his master's thesis, and the commentaries already germinating, to formulate the seed of his first critical book, were all directed toward a comprehensive poetics. And it does seem more than a little tactless of Crane to write in such deprecating terms of Williams, assert that Winters does not have the range of Williams, and urge Winters to take a more sanguine view of the *Fire Sequence*. There was a kind of innocence in Crane; it should have occurred to him, as it certainly did to Winters, that the *Fire Sequence* and *The Bridge* were parallel if not competing works. On September 15 of 1928, Winters wrote to Tate that the *Fire Sequence* had attempted a synthesis of more diverse materials than *The Bridge,* and that if it fell short of Crane's work, that was because of Crane's genius, not Winters's conception. At this moment, Winters was too unsure of his work and its directions to make any defense.

Crane sent 'O Carib Isle" to *transition,* and it appeared in the April issue. The magazine became a major supporter of Crane's work; of the nineteen poems published in 1927, eight appeared in *transition.* This would be important to him as ingress to the Parisian expatriates when he spent his difficult period there in 1929.

The next letter must have been incomprehensible to Winters — why should Crane expect his typewriter to speak Spanish? The incident has been reported in full in Unterecker,[3] though some details differ from the account in this letter. Crane was attempting to write a letter expressing his admiration for Plutarco Calles, president of Mexico. Calles was much in the news in early 1927 because he had acted on land reform and, among other radical changes, had enacted in 1925 and then enforced a law requiring all non-Mexican holders of oil rights to exchange those rights for fifty-year leases. Except for American oil companies, there were no complaints, but Secretary of State Kellogg looked on this provocation as grounds for possible American armed intervention; to him, Calles — in fact a liberal nationalist — was a Bolshevist. The weekly magazines that Crane read most closely because his friends contributed to them, *The Nation* and *The New Republic,* ran editorials and feature articles defending Calles and demanding that there be no war with Mexico. They were not being hysterical; the Marines were at that time in Nicaragua. The title page of *The Nation* for January 26 read simply, "No war with MEXICO," and the main editorial was titled "No, Mr. Coolidge — No!" This was characteristic of the tone of editorials and articles, especially by Carleton Beals, for the first months of 1927 in both magazines. Spurred by this general tone, after a night of friendly drinking, Crane urged all his friends to write to Calles and went home to hold up his end of the scheme. The bizarre results were generally close to those reported by Winters.

Patterson
March 27

Dear Winters:

You'll have to bear with the calamities of my penmanship for awhile, as I got drunk on some neighborhood vintage the other night, started to write a letter of sympathy to President Calles, found that the typewriter did not speak adequate Spanish — and hurled it from the window. As I always write from high latitudes there wasn't much left of the machine after it hit the ground. My old gammer of a landlady reports that while I did not strike her she was nevertheless swept to the floor in attempting to restrain me from throwing the lamp also out the window — and that we both lay on the floor for some time afterward while I howled imprecations against Coolidge, etc. Since which I have been working on the River section of P's Daughter — and have felt in some ways much better. Even the eyes have improved — though I'm doing practically no reading.

The first issue of *transition* arrived yesterday. It is far better constructed — physically and "spiritually" than I expected. I have a vague conviction that it [is] going to live the superhuman term of at least a year. And it so intrigues me that I'm going to send Jolas a number of things — regardless of payment — which is negligible especially in view of the fact that being printed in France one can still market here and England also, from all I know. The magazine somehow bespeaks a larger audience for our kind of work than I had suspected despite the fact that *transition* includes a number of soft spots and "softies" — but you can't say more for any U.S.A. periodical that I know of. The New Republic poetry is controlled by a male Miss who won't even take tea because it's too "stimulating" — and The Dial is so "nice" — well! But they've just taken P's D. (4 pages) and Aunt Harriet has just taken Cutty Sark — so I'm not in half the rage today that I've been possessed of for so long. But I think *transition* is a good wedge to use — and I hope it appeals to you somewhat as it does to me. The version of Carib Isle which has appeared therein is slightly different than the version which appears in Poetry — which is again slightly different from the version as it will appear in the Calendar! Hurricanes seem to take with editors — or is it Carib mathematics — at any rate if there were only more Anglicized countries in the world that poems might pay my way around it!

I think that the Indian chieftain's name is all the better for not being particularly definite — especially as Pocahontas had a thousand Indian lovers for the one white marriage license to the English planter. I shall continue to depend on taxi drivers for all matters of folklore. And thank you much for the invaluable check-up, which at least reassures me that the name didn't mean Rosenphallus or Hot Tomaly . . .

Your observation as regards Tate comes at an "interesting" time. I'm worried about him: not his theories so much as their effects on him. They seem to be discouraging his production — but this may be only a passing phase, due more to the gagging circumstances that beset all of us.

Don't worry too much about your book: publishers are always devilishly slow about poetry. Mine was "in the press" nearly eight months. Ms claimed "lost," etc. etc. But keep agitating! I sent you off an awful lot of maudlin theoretical sentiment in my last. I hope you haven't felt it deserved much concern. Some day I'll get down to some formulations — but the present is too clouded and crowded by (everyday) some fresh problem.

Best to you,
Hart Crane

P.S. I'm glad Van Winkle "went" with you. And the first two songs. You do brace me up! Wait till you see the briefer on White Bldgs in the Dial! I'm accused of intellectual faking—it somehow "got sent" along with proofs of P's D. I don't know when it will appear.

Work on "The River" did not progress, and it would be July before Crane had it in finished enough state to show it to Winters. Crane got what satisfaction he could from the capitulation of editors to the work of the previous year and Winters's approval of two of the "Three Songs" and the "Van Winkle" section of *The Bridge*. Their mutual concern about Tate came from his hesitations and doubts, especially his doubts about the possibility of writing important poetry in an age without any grand agreed system of accounting for the phenomena. From Winters's point of view Tate had put himself in the position of writing poetry about the impossibility of writing great poetry. Since he could not accept Winters's "primitive" position derived from Amerindian poetry and Williams, he was committed to willful decadence. So Winters had written to Tate on March 19, and it is interesting that Winters already saw the options of modernist poetry oscillating between (what was to be the title of his first critical book) primitivism and decadence.

Winters was going through the common agony of poets, waiting for a publisher to get busy on a book, *The Bare Hills*. The briefer in *The Dial* was hardly flattering:

Mr Allen Tate, in a eulogistic preface to Mr Hart Crane's volume of verse, expresses a fear lest "his style may check the immediate currency of the most distinguished American poetry of the age." He remarks also: "Crane's poems are a fresh vision of the world, so intensely personalized in a new creative language that only the strictest and most unprepossessed effort of attention can take it in." After this, a sufficiently unprepossessed effort of attention becomes difficult. Mr Crane has ability: he makes good phrases, and is capable of writing excellent blank verse; but he seldom writes a completely satisfactory poem. Partly this is due to certain affec-

tations of idiom, to a straining and self-conscious and disin-
genuous preciosity; partly it is perhaps occasioned by an un-
reflecting indulgence in what one might call high-class intellectual fake. When Mr Crane writes less pretentiously, he is
more successful, as In Shadow and the second part of Voyages. The latter has great beauty, both of colour and movement.[4]

Including it with the proofs of Crane's "The Dance" was another
thrust in the hostility between Marianne Moore and Crane that
had grown up from the fuss about "The Wine Menagerie."

But whatever annoyance the briefer might have stirred was
quickly alleviated. Winters's review finally appeared in the April
Poetry, a reminder of the loyal support Crane had from Winters
and Tate. Crane's gratitude was expressed in the genuinely
charming collage he sent to Winters, who kept it on his study wall
throughout his life; he thought it exquisite.

Patterson
April 2 '27

Dear Winters:

I'm sending you a little two-dimensional toy it amused me to
make one sunshiny day — and if "he" arrives in any kind of condition you will probably not notice the *complete* extent of his tinni-
ness and overstuffing. "Musician Apostolic" is his name — and he
descends a mountain with a halo and guitar or fiddle — which in-
struments, I hope, won't [illegible] in transit!

I began drawing and puppet-ing at five and never have quite
got over it. Don't bother to keep this freak if it bores you. . . . For
awhile it amused me as a kind of idol mecanique, i.e. I seemed to
see it go through certain changes and "performances" as the light
would strike it one way or another. Your *Snow Ghost* does much
the same under different readings.

Your review has just reached me. You and Tate have more
courage than any ten other men I could pick. What laurels! It is
so extremely well written that it almost seems as though Aunt

Harriet's little note of warning turned, or were turned, into applause. Honored is no word for what I feel!

I've been playing the Indian dances—and like them *almost* as well as some Carib-Cubano things I have. Yes—please do send me photos of the "Polelonemo" pictures some time. You'd like some African stuff I have hung around here—wooden knives & ceremonial spear, shield, headdress, libation cup, viol—etc.

> *Hastily*
> *Hart Crane*

Crane's musician arrived in good condition, though the gelatine cloud at the top had become detached. Winters wrote to Crane asking exactly where in the construct the gelatine should be placed, thanking him heartily for the loveliness of the collage. Ironically, in so literary a correspondence, the only surviving letter from Winters to Crane concerns this visual artifact. Winters wanted to preserve it, for itself, and as a tangible connection with Crane, and asked whether framing it with glass would disturb the effect. He did manage a paragraph on literature: he had been reading Joyce's work in progress in *transition,* had worked out a way of coping with its language, found Joyce the oddest genius in literary history, and was bewildered that Tate could not see Joyce's work as major. For Winters, Joyce was one more proof of the greatness of the literary period that he and Crane inhabited.

Crane replied from Cleveland, where he was at the end of a happy stay with his father and giving his mother what support he could as she went through the last stages of her second divorce. There was no paper to write on except Winters's letter; hence its survival.

> *April 18—Cleveland*

Dear Winters: Am leaving for Patterson tonight—after a mad harrowing two-weeks with the bevy of my family. Divorces, illness, nervous breakdowns, litigation — so I'm tired and much "re-duced." Both your good letters have just been forwarded to me here, and I'm using this one in lieu of other paper around here.

I've marked the position of the gelatine cloud as near as I can remember it — but I may be wrong. The vertical line is the center of the page and the horizontal the top of the black mat-back-ground. Glad you like it. I had glass over it — and if it's worth the cost of framing I don't think the glass will spoil it.

When I get back to the woods I'll compose myself to a better letter. Meanwhile please forgive haste, etc. I haven't had a moment to myself for ages, it seems!

Faithfully,
Hart Crane

Winters responded to the gift by sending Crane photographs of paintings by Polelonema, a Hopi artist that he had met in Santa Fe. After the tiring visit to Cleveland, Crane took particular plea-sure in the work, especially since Winters had used a phrase in his poem for the painter in describing the quality of Crane's imagery. Winters purchased several of Polelonema's smaller portraits for two dollars apiece; he did not have the money to buy one of the larger complicated canvases that he and Janet Lewis so greatly admired. The photographs sent to Crane grew from Winters's having had copies made of the works to interest the editors of *transition* in printing them. Winters was so taken by the artist that he continued sending him paper and brushes from Palo Alto, items hard to come by on Indian reservations.

Although Crane could write an account of what he had so far done on *The Bridge,* the emotional turmoil of dealing with his parents left him with inadequate energy for working seriously on "The River." He sent Winters the last two sections of *The Bridge,* finished some time before. Later, in reviewing the whole poem, Winters would take a dim view of "The Tunnel" and "Atlantis." Crane's letter prefigures the possibility of those objections. The correspondence does not show that Winters made any comment on this body of poetry before his public expression of dislike.

Patterson, NY
April 29th '27

Dear Winters:

I got back here over a week ago, but have hardly yet settled down or managed to collect myself for any thought or occupation. However, I have all summer to plan on, that is, if there isn't too damned much weekending and visiting around the neighborhood. Much talk tires me terribly: and that is what Cleveland and my relatives, sick or well, always accomplish on my visits there!

Yesterday came the two delightful Polelonemas. They are already perched on my walls. The female figure seems so far to be the more original, but what lovely feet they both have! Yes, they are truly "seeds no sparrow cracks" — and the kind of thing that time helps you to further appreciate. Your Hartley image was vastly amusing. I've met Hartley a couple of times, admiring his painting (mainly for color) — and can readily recognize the amazing physiognomy of the original.

Enclosed are the last two sections of the Bridge, parts of which I am still somewhat anxious about, most notably the first page of the Tunnel. Yet I may have to leave it largely as it is, for the rawness of the subject necessarily demands a certain sort of sensitizing introduction — which, if it savors a little of Eliot and his 'wistfulness,' seems nevertheless indispensable toward the fixation or due registration of the subsequent developments of the theme. I flatter myself that I drop off the Eliot mood quite a ways before Chambers Street. And I venture to think that you will like the various throwbacks to Part I, and the Columbus theme.

As for the Atlantis — I imagine it to be too subjectively written for me to legitimately explain or condone. It was the first part of the poem to be written — and that in a kind of three-days fit, the memory alone of which is enough to justify it with me. I have later discovered that it contains a metaphysical synthesis of a number of things like aeronautics, telegraphy, psychoanalysis, atomic theory, relativity, and what not! It aspires a little (perhaps far too much!) to the famous Pater-ian 'frozen music,' i.e. it may rely too much on a familiarity with the unique architecture of Brooklyn Bridge, to me the most superb and original example of an American architecture yet hinted at, albeit accidentally; and I may have to ask all willing readers to take a walk across same to get the marvelous feeling the webbed cables give (as one advances) of a simultaneous forward and upward motion. In any case Atlantis stands or falls as my synthesized version of the poem as a Whole.

I should perhaps apologize for the apparently affected device of the quotation preceding each section: it is my hope that such a device may possibly alleviate the by-now chronic bewilderment of my *general* reader! Section One has the famous lines from Seneca's Medea (Ultima Thule, etc.); II, the lines quoted from some colonial chronicle about Pocahontas 'wheeling the boyes,' etc.; Three Songs takes a line from Hero & Leander; and so on. . . . I can hardly resist mentioning that all the place-names in the Tunnel actually do exist, and I honestly regard it as something of a miracle that they happened to fall into the same kind of symbolical functioning as the boat-names took in Cutty Sark.

I have never been to Floral Park nor Gravesend Manor, but you do actually take the 7th Avenue Interborough to get there, and you change for same at Chambers Street. A boozy truckdriver I used to talk with a good deal in a lowdown dive lived out there, used to talk about the girls 'shaping up,' and finally died at Floral Park, Flatbush. There are some new timbres and tonalities, I think, in the Tunnel — at least if I know what nearly maddened me for three years until I got a few of the acid tremors down on paper — if I have!

Don't strain your good will trying to like these sections: I shall be glad if you give me a few shots where the main failings are.

> *Faithfully yours,*
> *Hart Crane*

Crane had fallen deeply and happily in love. The young man was intelligent and cultivated, appreciative of Crane's qualities, and, within the limits of the affair, devoted to him. Crane met the young man on May 4, and when his monthly fifty dollars arrived from his father, he wrote to Wilbur Underwood on May 12:

I'm going in for the weekend to see Phoebus Apollo again. I quote the close of a letter just received: 'If you are in the city I should like very much to see you. I cannot come to you; for the last silver dollar is squandered and gone. Yet omnia vincit amor. It is a little life and tomorrow—we may die. Dum vivimus, vivamus. May I see you? A morte . . .'

He is in the quartermaster's div. and has brains as well as beauty and ———!⁵

In spite of his friend's protestations, he did accompany Crane to Patterson about the time of Crane's next letter to Winters:

Patterson, NY
May 21, 1927

Dear Winters:

Thanks immensely for your letter—and especially for the *retrato*. It occurred to me that an exchange of countenances might approximate in some ways the meeting in NY which we had—for awhile—expected this year.

I take it you are about to abandon Moscow to plunge into new macrocosms. It is a stimulating prospect. . . . As for me—I am disabled from everything but the alphabet, having fallen anew into love this spring. Nothing can now be expected from me but a little hoeing in the garden, though I am still active enough to anticipate the comments you promise on the Atlantis, etc.

I'm glad to hear that your book is in active hands and will be out soon. I'm sending for it—and if I feel at all sufficiently capable I shall essay a review for transition (the only editor who seems to have an ounce of confidence in anything I say).

I hope to have the 3rd section of P's Daughter (The River) done soon. There's so much to be done yet! I'm really in a bad mood! Will write more later when I'm a bit less dizzy.

Best always,
Hart Crane

The exchange of portraits (see facing page) and the offer to review Winters's *The Bare Hills* continued the amicable relations between the two men. Winters pasted Crane's photograph on the inside front cover of his copy of *White Buildings*. But in a little over a week a letter from Crane would come close to destroying the friendship.

Hart Crane, 1926

Yvor Winters, 1928

V

A THREATENING LETTER

The following letter is the only one of the forty-six extant letters from Crane to Winters that has had any currency; it was quoted in Crane's first biography; it is quoted in full in the *Letters* and in Unterecker. The original was kept in the Crane-Winters papers, but Crane made an accurate carbon. Since it is the only letter to Winters widely known, and since it chimes with many prejudices about Winters, it was held a prominent place in judgments of the relation between the two poets. Actually, its direction is dual, toward Winters and toward Edmund Wilson. The occasions were a letter from Winters and an omnibus review of the poetry of the past year by Wilson in *The New Republic*. The "good drubbing" Winters deserves is, by implication, also offered to Wilson. Winters's letter is lost, but it seems evident that he was volunteering moral counsel to Crane on sexual and literary matters, the first indication that Winters had overstepped the basic common ground of poetics and general friendly discourse. Wilson says nothing in his review about sexual matters; Winters seems to have been guilty of a serious gaffe. Crane neither wanted nor required direction in the intimate details of his life. Winters had before him the letter about Calles, indicating drunkenness and violence on Crane's part, the vague note about Crane's being in love, and the disappointing lack of productiveness on the main project of *The Bridge*. Winters was also dissatisfied on receiving "The Tunnel" and "Atlantis," seeing in the first the Eliotic qualities that he had come to consider the bane of current poetic concerns and in the second the inexact poetic verbiage that, in Winters's final judgment, made *The Bridge* in many respects a disaster. Considering the quality and quantity of work on *The Bridge* which had come to Winters's attention in the past few months, except for the "Three Songs," he had reason to be troubled.

Crane was not the only poet annoyed by Wilson's review; he managed to say offensive things about practically every poet writing, from James Rorty to T. S. Eliot, with the exception of Edna Millay, his intimate friend. When Wilson reprinted the essay in *The Shores of Light,* he included part of Crane's letter, along with complaints from John Crowe Ransom and others. Crane fared rather well: "When one looks back on the American poetry of the season, one is aware of only two events which emerge as of the first interest: *The King's Henchman,* by Miss Millay, and *White Buildings,* by Mr. Hart Crane."[1] This at least set Crane above Ransom, Damon, Bodenheim, MacLeish, and Van Doren. He grants Crane a voice of considerable range, and he concedes him grandeur of style, and then takes away the grandeur immediately:

> Mr. Crane has a most remarkable style, a style which is strikingly original — almost something like a great style, if there could be such a thing as a great style which was, not merely not applied to a great subject, but not, so far as one can see, applied to any subject at all.[2]

The comparison with Rimbaud grants that poetry need not have any clear continuity of image or idea, but with Rimbaud, after all the fireworks, "we divine what he is saying."[3] Crane remains curiously vague. His poetry is like a soldier on unattached duty:

> We are eagerly waiting to see to which part of the front he will move it: just at present, it is killing time in the cafés behind the lines.[4]

Phrases like this stung, but there was more.

Current American poetry, Wilson argued, suffered from the poets' lack of social function, in contrast to Waller, Milton, and Prior. Wilson thought the poet ill advised to give up all for the Muse, "to seclude himself in the country, to live from hand to mouth in Greenwich Village or to escape to the Riviera." The Riviera was not accessible to Crane, but he was living in isolation in Patterson and could at most expect to gain in New York just the marginal existence that Wilson proscribes. No wonder Crane was upset: the style of his poetry was praised and damned in one sentence; his manner of life was condemned in another. And what could he do about it? Piled on Wilson's assertion and denial of his merit as a poet came a letter from a man upon whom he looked as an ally casting gratuitous moral doubts on his private conduct. The concept of the whole man became a personal insult. Further, though exact dates are hard to determine, his especially happy and successful love affair with the sailor had come to its inevitable end—ships do not stay in port forever, and this reminder of the instability of his erotic life was aggravated by Winters's letter. What was in the letter? Comments on Leonardo, probably connecting the fragmentary accomplishments of that great genius with his sexual identity, and certainly some animadversions of the inconsecutive slow conduct of Crane's work on *The Bridge*. In his sometimes blundering affability, Winters might well have thought that the comparison of Crane with Leonardo was hardly an insult. Judging from Winters's letters to Tate, he could breach tact rather easily in his correspondence. He certainly touched off an explosion in Crane.

Patterson, New York
May 29th, 1927

Dear Winters:
    You need a good drubbing for all your recent easy talk about 'the complete man,' the poet and his ethical place in society, etc. I'm afraid I lack the time right now to attempt what I might call a relatively complete excuse for committing myself to the above

sentiments — and I am also encumbered by a good deal of sympathy with your viewpoint in general. Wilson's article was just half-
baked enough to make one warm around the collar. It is so
damned easy for such as he, born into easy means, graduated
from a fashionable university into a critical chair overlooking
Washington Square, etc. to sit tight and hatch little squibs of
advice to poets not to be so 'professional' as he claims they are, as
though all the names he has just mentioned had been as suavely
nourished as he — as though 4 out of 5 of them hadn't been
damned well forced the major part of their lives to grub at *any*
kind of work they could manage by hook or crook and the fear of
hell to secure! Yes, why not step into the State Dept. and join the
diplomatic corps for a change! indeed, or some other courtly
occupation which would bring you into wide and active contact
with world affairs! As a matter of fact I'm all too ready to concede
that there are several other careers more engaging to follow than
that of poetry. But the circumstances of one's birth, the conduct
of one's parents, the current economic structure of society and a
thousand other local factors have as much or more to say about
successions to such occupations, the naive volitions of the poet to
the contrary. I agree with you of course, that the poet should in as
large a measure as possible adjust himself to society. But the question always will remain as to how far the conscience is justified in
compromising with the age's demands.

The image of 'the complete man' is a good idealistic antidote
for the horrid hysteria for specialization that inhabits the modern
world. And I strongly second your wish for some definite ethical
order. Munson, however, and a number of my other friends, not
so long ago, being stricken with the same urge, and feeling that
something must be done about it — rushed into the portals of the
famous Gurdjieff Institute and have since put themselves through
all sorts of Hindu antics, songs, dances, incantations, psychic ses-
sions, etc. so that now, presumably the left lobes of their brains
and their right lobes respectively function (M's favorite word) in
perfect unison. I spent hours at the typewriter trying to explain to
certain of these urgent people why I could not enthuse about
their methods; it was all to no avail, as I was told that the 'com-

plete man' had a different logic than mine, and further that there was no way of gaining or understanding this logic without first submitting yourself to the necessary training. I was finally left to roll in the gutter of my ancient predispositions, and suffered to receive a good deal of unnecessary pity for my obstinance. Some of them, having found a good substitute for their former interest in writing by means of more complete formulas of expression have ceased writing now altogether, which is probably just as well. At any rate they have become hermetically sealed souls to my eyesight, and I am really not able to offer judgment.

I am not identifying your advice in any particular way with theirs, for you are certainly logical, so much so that I am inclined to doubt the success of your program even with yourself. Neither do you propose such paradoxical inducements as tea-dansants on Mt. Everest! I am only begging the question, after all, and asking you not to judge me too summarily by the shorthand statements that one has to use as the makeshift for the necessary chapters required for more explicit and final explanations. I am suspect, I fear, for equivocating. But I cannot flatter myself into quite as definite recipes for efficiency as you seem to, one reason being, I suppose, that I'm not so ardent an aspirant toward the rather classical characteristics that you cite as desirable. This is not to say that I don't 'envy' the man who attains them, but rather that I have long since abandoned *that* field—and I doubt if I was born to achieve (with the particular vision) those richer syntheses of consciousness which we both agree in classing as supreme; at least the attitude of a Shakespeare or a Chaucer is not mine by organic rights, and why try to fool myself that I possess that type of vision when I obviously do not!

I have a certain code of ethics. I have not as yet attempted to reduce it to any exact formula, and if I did I should probably embark on an endless tome with monthly additions and digressions every year. It seems obvious that a certain decent carriage and action is a paramount requirement in any poet, deacon or carpenter. And though I reserve myself the pleasant right to define these standards in a somewhat individual way, and to shout and complain when circumstances against me seem to warrant it, on the other hand I believe myself to be speaking honestly when I say that I have never been able to regret — for long — whatever has happened to me, more especially those decisions which at times have been permitted a free will. (Don't blame me entirely for bringing down all this simplicity on your head — your letter almost solicits it!) And I am as completely out of sympathy with the familiar whimpering caricature of the artist and his 'divine rights' as you seem to be. I am not a Stoic, though I think I could learn more in that direction if I came to (as I may sometime) appreciate more highly the imaginative profits of such a course.

You put me in altogether too good company, you compliment me much too highly, for me to offer the least resistance to your judgments on the structure of my work. I think I am quite unworthy of such associates as Marlowe or Valéry — except in some degree, perhaps, 'by kind.' If I can avoid the pearly gates long enough I may do better. Your fumigation of the Leonardo legend is a healthy enough reaction, but I don't think your reasons for doubting his intelligence and scope very potent. — I've never closely studied the man's attainments or biography, but your argument is certainly weakly enough sustained on the sole prop of his sex — or lack of such. One doesn't have to turn to homosexuals to find instances of missing sensibilities. Of course I'm sick of all this talk about balls and cunts in criticism. It's obvious that balls are needed, and that Leonardo had 'em — at least the records of the Florentine prisons, I'm told, say so. You don't seem to realize that the whole topic is something of a myth anyway, and is consequently modified in the characteristics of the image by each age in each civilization. Tom Jones, a character for whom I have the utmost affection, represented the model in 18th Century England, at least so far as the stated requirements of your letter would suggest, and for an Anglo-Saxon model he is still pretty good aside from calculus, the Darwinian theory, and a few other mental additions. Incidentally I think Tom Jones (Fielding himself, of course) represents a much more 'balanced' attitude toward society and life in general than our friend, Thomas Hardy. Hardy's profundity is real, but it is voiced in pretty much one monotonous key. I think him perhaps the greatest technician in

English verse since Shakespeare. He's a great poet and a mighty man. But you must be fanatic to feel that he fulfills the necessary 'balanced ration' for modern consumption. Not one of his characters is for one moment allowed to express a single joyous passion without a footnote of Hardian doom entering the immediate description. Could Hardy create anything like Falstaff? I think that Yeats would be just as likely—more so.

That's what I'm getting at. . . . I don't care to be credited with too wholesale ambitions, for as I said, I realize my limitations, and have already partially furled my flag. The structural weaknesses which you find in my work are probably quite real, for I could not ask for a more meticulous and sensitive reader. It is my hope, of course, not only to improve my statement but to extend scope and viewpoint as much as possible. But I cannot trust to so methodical and predetermined a method of development, not by any means, as you recommend. Nor can I willingly permit you to preserve the assumption that I am seeking any 'shortcuts across the circle,' not willfully excluding any experience that seems to me significant. You seem to think that experience is some commodity—that can be sought! One can respond only to certain circumstances, just what the barriers are, and where the boundaries cross can never be completely known. And the surest way to frustrate the possibility of any free realization is, it seems to me to willfully direct it. I can't help it if you think me aimless and irresponsible. But try and see if you get such logical answers always from Nature as you seem to think you will! My 'alert blindness' was a stupid ambiguity to use in any definition—but it seems to me you go in for just about as much 'blind alertness' with some of your expectations.

If you knew how little of a metaphysician I am in the scholastic sense of the term you would scarcely attribute such a conscious method to my poems (with regard to that element) as you do. I am an utter ignoramus in that whole subject, have never read Kant, Descartes or other doctors. It's all an accident so far as my style goes. It happens that the first poem I ever wrote was too dense to be understood, and now I find that I can trust most critics to tell me that all my subsequent efforts have been equally futile. Having heard that one writes in a metaphysical vein the usual critic will immediately close his eyes or stare with utter complacency at the page — assuming that black is black no more and that the poet means anything but what he says. It's as plain as day that I'm talking about war and aeroplanes in the passage from F & H (corymbulous formations of mechanics, etc) quoted by Wilson in the New Republic, yet by isolating these lines from the context and combining them suddenly with lines from a totally different poem he has the chance (and uses it) to make me sound like a perfect ninny. If I'd said that they were Fokker planes then maybe the critic would have had to notice the vitality of the metaphor and its pertinence. All this ranting seems somehow necessary. . . . If I am metaphysical I am content to continue so. Since I have been 'located' in this category by a number of people I may as well go on alluding to certain (what are also called) metaphysical passages in Donne, Blake, Vaughan, etc. as being of particular appeal to me on a basis of common characteristics with what I like to do in my own poems, however little scientific knowledge of the subject I may have.

I write damned little because I am interested in recording certain sensations, very rigidly chosen, with an eye for what according to my taste and sum of prejudices seems suitable to — or intense enough — for verse. If I were writing in prose, as I sometime shall probably do, I should probably include a much thicker slice of myself — and though it is the height of conceit for me to suggest it, I venture to say that you may have received a somewhat limited idea of my interests and responses by judging me from my poems alone. I suppose that in regard to this limitation of poetic focus one should consult the current position of poetry in relation to other intellectual and political characteristics of the time, including a host of psychological factors which may or may not promote the fullest flowering of a particular medium such as verse. I am not apologizing. Nor am I trying to penetrate beyond a certain point into such labyrinths of conjecture and analysis. It seems unprofitable. One should be somewhat satisfied if one's work comes to approximate a true record of such moments of 'illumination' as are occasionally possible. A sharpening of reality accessible to the poet, to no such degree possible through other mediums. That is one reason above all others—why I shall never expect (or indeed desire) *complete* sympathy from any writer of such originality as yourself. I may have neglected to say that I admire your general attitude, including your distrust of metaphysical or other patent methods. Watch out, though, that you don't strangulate yourself with some countermethod of your own!

Best wishes,
Hart Crane

How could one respond to such a letter? Crane after all his protestations of amiability had an instinct for the jugular vein, which he exercised. Winters wrote two letters in response and received a laconic note in reply.

Patterson
June 14th, '27

Dear Winters:
Please pardon my neglect of your two recent letters. I'm in a 'state' of writing again—and am deferring other matters for the time being. Also there has been gardening, guests and week-end parties.... I'll soon have the River section done, I think—and I'll send it on.

All best, hastily
HCrane

Crane continued to hold Winters at arm's length. His overt excuses were hay fever and new work on "The River." But the friendliness returned, the anxiety to share literary delights, *Arabia Deserta,* and a renewal of their common concern with contemporary poetry. Winters might very well have read the Wilson

essay that had in part occasioned Crane's diatribe; he did ask
Crane about three of the poets mentioned by Wilson. The letter
on "contemporary tragic poetic action" which Crane says he has
written seems to have gone astray or perhaps not to have been
kept by Winters. Winters during this period was concerned with
the possibilities of writing poetic drama, especially in free verse,
and he wrote at some length to Tate on the subject on June 23.
The alternative was a direct and stripped lyric form in free verse,
taking off from the few poems in *Fire Sequence* which Winters
still liked: "Liberation," "November," "The Bitter Moon." But
Winters was not satisfied with his work and had once again the
sense that he might not be able to go on as he had in the past, his
admiration for Shakespeare's sonnets calling into question his
own work and indeed all poetry.

Patterson
June 25th '27

Dear Winters:

I'm such a driveling gale of sneezing profanity and hay fever
lately I still can't write. I have got to find a location where I'll
escape this really serious malady—sometime before long—or I'm
afraid I'll have some chronic result like asthma saddled on me.
The sea is one answer, of course, and I guess there are lots of
places abroad—how about the Southwest where you are now? I
can't imagine much pollen near the desert.

Work on the River has been halted, of course. When my eyes
are able I'm reading *on* Doughty's Arabia Deserta. I don't think
I'll ever finish the 1100 or odd pgs. Have you read it? I'm anxious
to know because I think it a very great book, despite present fad,
almost as noisy as Mah Jong was, of praising it.

I don't know that I should advise you to buy Damon, Ransom
or Riding, though I feel guilty in more than one sense,—should
anyway, whichever advice I offered. All are amusing, however. It
just depends on what you want from them. Laura is so obscure
half the time I can't make much out. Notice how she carried her

metaphysical paradoxes (altogether too stylistically) into her criticism of Stein in the transition article: it's getting painfully mechanical I fear.

As I said, this is no answer to your admirable correspondence of the 4th. . . . But my brains are oozing down fiery pipes and my nose is skinned from efforts at tidiness. Your search for a convincing ethic for contemporary tragic poetic action illuminates all your previous remarks, and makes my last long letter (anent same) seem rather superfluous and trifling, I think.

all best—
Hart Crane

P.S. I sent the letter on to Tate, as you requested. But as we have become rather estranged, I'd rather not correspond further for the present.

Winters continued to send Crane photographs of Indian art, and finally Crane had finished "The River" and could send him a copy.

Patterson
July 1, '27

Dear Winters:

Thanks immensely for the marvelous crow-pole—or whatever the lovely Indian painting be called.

Here is the River, my long struggle with an attempt to tell the pioneer experience backward! I'll tell you more about other things I try to do in it—after I give you a chance to form your own impressions without my ego bristling all over the page. Excuse this crazy sentence—the postman is speeding over the hill and I'm simply spattering the page, I fear.

All best to you and to your wife—
Hart Crane

The dry climate of New Mexico, Winters felt, would check the onslaughts of hay fever that Crane suffered from, but Crane could not afford changing his residence—his economic position was worse than marginal. He was in a better frame of mind and less troubled by his allergies. He had not only finished "The River"—he could look on it critically and offer new versions of several lines. Winters wrote them into his copy of the poem. They were back on their more solid footing, exchanging poems, offering each other encouragement. I cannot find any trace of a poem by Winters called "Triumph," but at this stage in his life he was uncertain about his work and evidently questioned and destroyed a fair number of poems.

Patterson
July 5th, '27

Dear Winters:

I won't be able to utilize your generous inclinations to help me in the Southwest this summer, but I may next year, probably sometime, anyhow. I have always been curious about that section and shall surely make an effort to get there regardless of my malady, — which is disappearing now, leaving me much happier and with a relief that is almost exhilarating. Maybe getting the River done had something to do with it. Anyway that section had weighed so heavily on me for so long a period, and contained so many apparently insurmountable difficulties that I was becoming very depressed.

Since writing to you I have made the following emendations in such lines as the following:

High in a cloud of merriment recalled

—For early trouting. Then, etc

—Memphis to Tallahassee—riding the rods—
Blind fists of nothing, humpty-dumpty clods.

Papooses crying on the wind's long mane
Screamed redskin dynasties that fled the brain
— Dead echoes! etc.

Where eyeless fish curvet a sunken fountain

They doze now, below axe and powder horn.

And hum Deep River with them while they go

Yes, turn again and sniff once more — look see
O Sheriff, etc.

Dan Midland — jolted from the cold brake-beam.

They are very minor changes, but they sharpen the surface I think, and I feel justified in bothering you with them. I won't bore you with many of the almost countless considerations that made this section difficult — to tell the pioneer experience backward is the main intention, of course. To synthesize this with a simultaneous flow of the present, yet drive through the necessary contrasts presents a lot of problems. It is *timed* insofar as I have been able to time it, every word and beat is measured and weighed. I have done my best to slightly vary a continuous and (I think) desirable underlying monotony of rhythm — to carry it through a number of transitions and finally plant the entirety in the hieratic largo of the River.

Pocahontas is posited quite definitely as the "Body" of the soil. The tramps are simply interlocutors, psychological ponies. I do think this flows much more evenly than any piece of equal length that I've done before, its movement is different than any other part of the Bridge and I think that it forms an interesting contrast to the rapid foot-beat of the Dance that follows, makes a real foundation for it. I've tried to give it the racial tang of the Great Valley without lapsing into Sandburgian sentimentalities, but one can never be a judge of such considerations without the comments of others. I think that much of your recent criticism has helped me a good deal in guarding against some of my weaknesses, but it is a hopeless conceit to believe this until I get your comments! If my 'heat' continues, I'll soon have the Indiana section done, which will round up the map with the ocean again. (I have a 49er Indiana farmer saying goodbye to his son who is leaving for the sea.)

I haven't read Keyserling. After reading Spengler last summer under a tropic sun I have felt a little timid about further German adventures. It was only Don Quixote who pulled me up enough after Spengler to put me on the Bridge again! By all means read Doughty though, even the abbreviation which you have. What you should have is the whole work, however, even though you read only half of it. The thing can't be parcelled out without losing the aweful monotony and tragic observation.

I am sending you two recent numbers of The Calendar, London, which you can return to me sometime at your convenience. it is one of the few magazines I enjoy taking and in case these two numbers please you I am enclosing a subscription blank. Some of the reviews are especially good: read the review of "God, Man and Epic Poetry" by Rickword in the April no. Rickword likes my stuff and is bringing out the Three Songs in the forthcoming July number. Wish you would send him some of your poetry. By the way, the Dead Baby by Williams in transition is a perfect thing, perfect! It's heartening to see how he comes back every so often to something so solid and seriously performed. Why does he think he must forever fuss with some attenuated method of presentation, viz. most of his recent work in the Dial! I like the last things you sent me very much. They don't overtop such things as November and the Rows of Cold Trees however. I think Triumph is the best of them and superb.

affectionately yours,
Hart Crane

Winters was stirred by the poem. Even in his negative review of *The Bridge,* he singled out eight stanzas of it for praise, and he was by then not favorably disposed toward Crane's idea of the epic. On first reading, he approved "The River" wholeheartedly. Crane in response felt compelled to send "The Air Plant" and two other unidentified poems. "The Air Plant" is included in the papers, but the other two poems are not. Later, Crane would send Winters still more of the poems originating in his Caribbean experience. At last, when he had lost interest in it, Winters would see the publication of *The Bare Hills,* and Crane volunteered to review it, a balance for the review of *White Buildings.* Nothing came of this, but they were back on their old friendly ground.

Crane sent Winters an early version of "The Air Plant," dated July 12. The corrected version followed within a week. The initial version was accompanied by a note:

Dear Winters —
This is a relic of my sailing trip last summer — and is meant along with two or three others as a companion piece to Carib Isle.

HC

The second version had as a typed footnote "corrected version."

Patterson, NY
July 18th, '27

Dear Winters:
I can't tell you how your praise and approbation heartens me! Believe me, though, when I call myself most fortunate in having a reader who simply gets everything on the page! My expression is so limited today, due to a cyder spree with friends yesterday, that I'm not attempting much of a letter. I'll try to do better anon when I'm more 'assembled.' Meanwhile it is not my intention to allow you the least bit of rest!

Here is the corrected version of The Air Plant, as well as two other pieces recently written and belonging to the Carib suite that

I've been meditating. (It's rather good to get off The Bridge for awhile.) Two remain to be written, but I think I'll group them together under the common title of *The Hurricane*, beginning with

> O Carib Isle!
> Quarry
> Royal Palm
> The Idiot (still to be written)
> &Eternity (a description of the ruins)

with maybe one or two more items, as my tropical memories dictate.

I tried The River on The Dial, but it came back. Am trying The Nation now, where it will probably evoke just plain bewilderment. Glad to hear about your book. I want to write a review of it for *transition,* but I make such a mess of things whenever I try to formulate any sort of formal criticism! If I can't leave you as clean and direct as you are it'll go in the wastebasket.

all best,
Hart Crane

Two versions of "The Mermen" preceded the letter of August 3. The first is dated July 26 with the following note:

Dear Winters: Think you will like this. The coincidence of the quotation is scarcely credible: after writing the last line I dipped into *Lear,* and, believe me or no—that's the first line I saw! Will try to write a decent letter soon.

all best
Hart Crane

The second is dated July 27, with another note:

Dear Winters: Forgive my premature combustions! These eidolons are awful snarls—their damned multiplicity of suggestion!

yrs
Hart Crane

There would be a long interruption in the correspondence from August to November, rising from Crane's confused search for funds and employment. The correspondence temporarily ended with a characteristic letter praising some of Winters's recent work, scheming for a review of Winters's poetry, and enclosing a copy of "The Hurricane"—here titled "The Hour."

Patterson, NY
Aug. 3rd '27

Dear Winters:

Your experience with the turtles is a poem in itself! Or rather a dramatic poem. The frequent vigor of your prose descriptions— and a certain gift for anecdotal poignancy—makes me wish that you would cut loose in some prose work sometime, even if only the usual autobiography. Eyes as sharp as yours, and brains as sharply sane, would construct something memorably beyond the usual stage-whispered plaint.

I like Teeth of Hell immensely. It consummates the sum of impulses of half a dozen lesser poems of yours, and is in many ways the most essentialized Winters I've seen.

The
brain is drenched in speed, is
heavier and heavier, and God
is speed exceeding motion

is exactly what I have been trying to say more emotionally in the enclosed hurricane poem. By which I'm not implying that your

poem as a whole is any less emotional than I think mine, only that
the directions of the two poems are different. I am trying to give
only one impression—the terrific and limitless single blast of destruction, wherein even thunder is submerged. The terrific tom-
tom of that hurricane I won't soon forget.

You are quite right about the relative worth of the recent pieces
I've been doing. Most of them are all-too-near the kind of thing
that is just grabbed up for anthologies. A little proficiency is a
dangerous thing, and these things have just enough of that to
attain the so-so qualities in current demand. Reviving senses during the last few days have considerably clipped their stature, and
I am now in a kind of blue-funk—as much due to recent wet
weather, probably, as anything. And then—one ought to be away
from one's desk entirely for awhile. Poetry is better followed as an
avocation (I never have contended otherwise, despite my recent
outburst at Wilson, and were it not that I'm honor-bound to plug
away at this Bridge until I finish it, I'd hasten to practice once
again what I preach. Nothing is *easy*, of course, either way.

I read Whitehead's book some time ago, realizing that I was
getting only about 10 per cent of the gist of one page. My mind is
so untrained in those directions that I didn't even try to make up
my mind about the book. I have, however, come to about the
same conclusions regarding the present cul-de-sac of modern sciences and their drift that you voice in your letter. That's why, in
my rather blind way, I pitched into you for your seemingly wholesale adherence to the Loeb-biochemical theoretical stuff as adequate poetic theme, some months back. I can't sustain my prejudices very well in these fields, though. I can only admit both igno-
rance and prejudice, and at the same time claim a fair amount of
curiosity—as much as I can ever reasonably hope to satisfy without useless torture.

I forgot to mention the Darnel poem. This seems quite perfect,
solid (sometimes your poems are *too* solid, but this moves within
itself). The strange eloquence of the thing (especially as it
approaches the end) stays with one. Maybe my enthusiasm for
these two poems is premature, since I received them only this
morning, but I hardly think it will prove to be. I'll look up Tri-

umph, and make the alteration there directly. The Calendar definitely died with the July number. I regret it very much. I may send you an extra copy to keep. There were interesting items in't. Marianne isn't to blame for the River rejection — at least she's still in Europe on a vacation, so I hear. Burke is taking her place now, but has no definite authority. If Pound had only been made editor of the Dial years ago! The decrepit old wind bag goes wheezing along month after month with dear old Schnitzler and Mann the main bellows-workers. The dictatorship of London is divided between such as Eliot and Squire, the latter, dreadful as he is, in many ways preferable to the former — as literary dictator. Eliot long ago had heart-failure, but insists on you, as well as he, wearing your liver on your sleeve henceforth.

I have ordered your book from the publisher, but as yet have had no answer from them. I'm expecting to receive the book soon, however. I think I'll try a review on The Nation before *transition*. It would be better politics at least. Forgive my present dullard mood.

All best,
Hart Crane

Crane did not write to Winters again until November 23, when Crane would start his brief hectic California interlude, and the two men would finally meet.

VI

THEIR ONLY MEETING

That interval of silence on Crane's part embraced periods of crucial change for both poets. As Malcolm Cowley observed, the completion of "The River" marked the end of Crane's development as a poet;[1] and by summer of 1927, Winters had reached the end of his first period as an experimental writer. His entry that fall into the Stanford graduate school introduced him for the first time to systematic study of the history of English literature, and though Winters is justified in saying that Stanford did not cause the development toward his later style, that it grew from his personal sense of the inadequacy of his free verse experiments to the kind of poetry he genuinely admired, that of Baudelaire, Valéry, "and Hardy, Bridges, and Stevens in a few poems each"[2] the impact of William Dinsmore Briggs and of the canon of poetry in English were, in effect, Stanford.*

Early in summer Winters rejoined Janet Lewis Winters in Santa Fe, and they then went on to Palo Alto where they settled in a rustic atmosphere, with Winters's dogs, soon to be augmented by goats, and a sizable vegetable garden. Crane went through a series of abortive plans, hoping again to establish the conditions that led to the creative period on the Isle of Pines. At times he wanted to return to the island, but there was no real house to live in since the hurricane; he was impelled toward Martinique, then Mallorca, then Europe in general, or he would seek employment in New York. His father continued sending him fifty

*See appendix.

dollars a month, and in September he received a further subsidy of three hundred dollars from Otto Kahn.[3] Martinique seemed possible, but in mid-October his mother moved to Hollywood with his ailing grandmother, and she objected to his being so remote from her. He found an unsatisfying job in a bookstore in New York, and then in early November he was invited to act as secretary and companion to Herbert A. Wise, a wealthy man recovering from a nervous breakdown. Crane looked on the arrangement as the greatest possible luck. Wise was going to Altadena, California, so that Crane could see his mother frequently without bearing the full burden of her constant presence.

Winters was within reach by a twelve-hour train ride, and he was one of the first people that Crane wrote to, only two days after his arrival. At Winters's request he had visited Elizabeth Madox Roberts, whom Winters had known since his year at the University of Chicago in 1917-18. Winters had in fact contributed to her support while he was studying at Boulder and she was suffering from illness. The book that Crane had just finished reading was *My Heart and My Flesh*. The letter is dated November 23, 1927 from Mr. Wise's rented mansion at 2160 Mar Vista Ave. in Altadena.

> *2160 Mar Vista Ave.*
> *Altadena, Cal.*
> *November 23rd, 1927*

Dear Winters:

Ye Gods! what a pink vacuum this place around here is! I just arrived day before yesterday, and already I'm beginning to wish I had jumped off the train around Albuquerque. I sort of sensed it at the time—and almost did. The hybrid circumstances of my immediate environment make it all the worse: a millionaire neurotic (nice as he is) with valet, chauffeur, gardener, and all the rest. This house seems to be all bathrooms and bad furniture, about which my boss suffers about as much as I do, but apparently the president of the American Express, who rented it to him, isn't afflicted by anything. I have already limousined around enough to wince at the 'sculptural' advertising which you mentioned. If the bull that advertises some eating place were only a bit more gilded, not to say gelded, I'd approve of that one piece, however, as a symbol at least, of the whole shebang. Did some one say Spanish architecture?!!!!

I won't promise not to blow off more steam before seeing you — when you'll get aplenty — but this will do for now. I'll try to keep the home fires burning somewhere within me without exploding and thereby losing my job. They say that work is hard to find in California. . . .

Yes, I went to see Elizabeth Madox Roberts. It was certainly worthwhile, and she was most cordial, though I never felt that society could torture any human being so much before, without intending to. I thought of a sibyl writhing on a tripod. No one, with any amount of deliberation, could have so taken the part. But I doubt if I should have remained any longer than I did, regardless of a previous engagement that took me away within a half hour. We talked about you, California, her book. This latter I had hurriedly read a day or so before meeting her. There is no doubt about its permanence as a major accomplishment. And one feels the sense of form, a relentless pattern, from the 20th page or so right on to the terrific torture of the climax — and then the beautiful 'dying fall,' the unforgettable pathos of the obscene inscriptions in the w.c. It's a marvelous book. But I don't think it necessarily diminishes the stature of *Ulysses*. Its range is more limited, and its intentions are different. Formally, yes, of course — it is more solid. Such debates are useless, however, with our present lack of any absolute critical logos.

I'm a bit muddled, and may remain so for awhile, especially as my situation demands a good deal of egg-stepping here. But I'll do my best to avoid boring you, and with the avid hope that you will support me to some extent by whatever rages, deliberations, constations, etc. may seem worthwhile putting on paper for the nonce or otherwise. I ordered your book from Four Seas months ago; has it come out yet?

Faithfully,
Hart Crane

Winters responded by suggesting that they meet at Christmas while he and Janet Lewis were visiting Winters's parents near Pasadena and close to Altadena. Crane welcomed the opportunity to meet one of his most devoted admirers, and he looked forward to some literary conversation. The review of *White Buildings* by Marichalar had appeared in the February 1927 edition of *Revista de Occidente* (Madrid). As Crane wrote to Slater Brown, he anticipated the arrival of Janet and Yvor Winters as a real event. The formality of Mr. Wise's household had a dulling effect on him. Crane wrote gratefully and with hearty anticipation to Winters on December 8:

> *2160 Mar Vista Ave.*
> *Altadena*
> *Dec. 8th*

Dear Winters:
    I am anticipating your Christmas visit a great deal. Please do get in touch with me right away on your arrival: phone *Niagara 2684*. I have just located a court near here, where, if I am a great deal improved in my technique by that time, we may possibly have a game or so. Right now I'm lamentable.
    This locale is certainly growing on me. No, I'm not turning up my nose. For one thing I've been too much out of breath! Movie studios have so far occupied a good deal of the time, mainly owing to my boss's curiosity in that direction. And I've looked up a couple of minor constellations (Alice Calhoun and Robert Graves) whom I used to know in school in Cleveland. Your kind introductions have been unemployed so far—simply owing to the rush. The world is small. . . . Ran into a very pleasant fellow who used to know Tate at Vanderbilt, etc. Meanwhile I'm becoming gradually accustomed to the formalities of a broker's household. AND begin to worry a little about having too good a time—that is for the approbation of the muses.
    But I have at least read his copies of Richards' *Principles*—and Weston's *Ritual to Romance*. The former is damned good. I look

forward to a detailed talk with you about it. The latter is especially interesting as revealing to me my unconscious use in *The Bridge* of a number of time-honored symbols. Wise (my boss) has a substantial enough stack of good things to read to keep me busy for some time.

I'm enclosing a review of "W.B." which was a good while getting to me, but which opened a slight correspondence between author and critic, which, if I ever go to Spain for a visit, may be profitable. Marichalar writes the Madrid letter for the *Criterion*. Perhaps you're already familiar with his work, prolog to the trans. of Joyce's *Portrait*—, etc. I had Macauley send him a copy of the *Am. Caravan,* which, he says, interests him very much. I hope later to see what he writes about it in the *Revista de Occidente*. Please don't lose this clipping. I had to correct him about the Statue of Liberty. That was a gift from the great *République Française,* you know!

> *All best to you—*
> *Crane*

The meeting between Crane and Winters has excited some lurid imaginings, but it was in fact gentle and decorous. Later, Winters was to observe that Crane's appearance was not healthy when they met:

> I saw Crane during the Christmas week of 1927, when he was approximately 29 years old; his hair was graying, his skin had the dull red color with reticulated grayish traceries which so often goes with advanced alcoholism, and his ears and knuckles were beginning to look a little like those of a pugilist.[4]

What evidence Winters had of Crane's "somewhat violent emotional constitution" came largely from hearsay. During their only meeting, Crane behaved amicably and politely. There was no drinking; there were no unseemly incidents.

This information comes from Janet Lewis Winters. She and her husband traveled by train from Palo Alto to Los Angeles, and as she said recently, "That was a long trip in those days." They stayed at the home of Winters's parents in Flintridge, overlooking Pasadena, the setting of Winters's childhood:

> From the high terrace porch I watch the dawn.
> No light appears, though dark has mostly gone,
> Sunk from the cold and monstrous stone. The hills
> Lie naked but not light . . .
>
> This is my father's house, no homestead here
> That I shall live in, but a shining sphere
> Of glass and glassy moments, frail surprise,
> My father's phantasy of Paradise . . . [5]

Crane came to visit them in the afternoon. Janet Lewis was still convalescing from tuberculosis and was confined to bed each day until four o'clock. They had tea together in her room, and they talked, about California, about poetry. Crane stayed for dinner, and after dinner Winters's father took them for a drive down the famous Christmas Tree street in Pasadena, lined with deodars and decorated and lighted brilliantly for the season. Crane and Winters shared the back seat, and Crane gave a wildly vivid recitation of the new version of "The Hurricane," which Winters had seen in an earlier form. They met four times for extended periods during that Christmas week.

They talked poetry, and as Janet Lewis says, Crane was charming, as he often could be. The conversations were evidently like the letters, affectionate and respectful and amusing, but always turning toward the common ground of poetry. They argued about Blake, with Winters pointing out that Blake's "The Tyger" was composed of perceptions throughout. Winters also showed and read aloud to Crane from the Bridges edition of Hopkins, to Crane's delight.

Winters was a natural pedagogue and Crane a grateful audience and interlocutor. Winters went through a considerable body of French poetry with Crane, especially Baudelaire, Rimbaud, and Valéry, though as Janet Lewis recalls, he did not read *Ebauche d'un Serpent*. Crane had very little French, so that Winters translated passages. Janet Lewis's clear impression is that Crane would have had difficulty struggling through a poetic passage with a dictionary and that he must have got all his French through translations. With Winters's magnificent sense of the poetic line and his thorough control of the language—and his pedagogic patience—it was a revelation to Crane.

To Winters, the occasion was one of the abiding joys of his life. In his essay on "The Significance of *The Bridge* by Hart Crane or What Are We to Think of Professor X" written some twenty years after the Christmas meeting of 1927, Winters says:

> Professor X says, or since he is a gentleman and a scholar, he implies, that Crane was merely a fool, that he ought to have known better. But the fact of the matter is, that Crane was not a fool. I knew Crane, as I know Professor X, and I am reasonably certain that Crane was incomparably the more intelligent man. As to Crane's ideas, they were merely those of Professor X, neither better nor worse; and for the rest, he was able to write great poetry. In spite of popular and even academic prejudices to the contrary, it takes a very highly developed intelligence to write great poetry, even a little of it. So far as I am concerned, I would gladly emulate Odysseus, if I could, and go down to the shadows for another hour's conversation with Crane on the subject of poetry . . . [6]

So deeply did Winters remember those meetings in Flintridge and Altadena, and perhaps those meetings came to his mind when he picked up the letters from Crane and contemplated their destruction. And he may well have remembered those golden days of the late twenties when he could earnestly write to Crane that they were living in a great literary period. Whatever his final judgments of Crane, from his first reading of "For the Marriage of Faustus and Helen" he saw genius in him and felt his death as a tragic waste and loss.

During the reminder of the stay their talks continued in an atmosphere of mutual respect and trust. Winters left behind several of his own poems. Crane was overwhelmed by Hopkins and asked Samuel Loveman to find him a copy, even if it cost ten dollars — a large sum at that time for anyone in Crane's financial circumstances. And, as he often did, he commented on Winters's poems. The poems should have suggested to him that some basic changes were occurring in Winters's poetics. For one thing, they were sonnets, and during their correspondence to that time, Winters had been writing in free verse. After Winters left, Crane puzzled over the sonnets and made characteristic comments. His criticism of one sonnet might have been instrumental in changes that Winters made.[7] Winters was to say that he wrote the sonnets to annoy Crane, but he took them with some seriousness.

Winters sent a copy of Hopkins to Crane and continued sending Crane poems for comment, and he also wrote a letter defending Crane from an attack by Kay Boyle in *transition* for January 1928. The attack by Boyle was balanced by a fuzzy review of *White Buildings* by Laura Riding. Apparently Winters's visit invigorated Crane's interest in poetry: he was reading Phelps Putnam's *Trinc* and MacLeish's *Streets in the Moon,* and he was weaving a tortuous passage through Ramon Fernandez's *Messages,* with little reward. The following two letters discuss the problems raised by his reading and by the January issue of *transition*.

Jan. 10 1928
Altadena

Dear Winters:

I've had a devil of a time making up my mind about the four sonnets! They are certainly not without value, possibly great value for all I can say — for I have the suspicion that some of the more obdurate lines contain concepts well beyond my scope of detection. My only complaint is that in general they strike me as but partially achieved "as harmoniously functioning units." . . . Why not work on them for a while longer, or lay them aside only, and take them up again! They have a fine, hard ring. Metrically good. But too skeletal—i.e. like a chemical formula rather than its concrete demonstration, which is an equivalent for what a poem ought to be in terms of metaphor. I have the idea that my "Atlantis" is lacking in the same sense.

"The winter stars flash into ermine dusk"—this sonnet strikes me as the best of them all, excepting perhaps "God in his loneliness—." There are as brilliant lines in others, but not as consistent a synthesis. For instance: "Screaming eternity of infinite logic is grinding down receding cold"... This blurs somehow. But there is perhaps no finer moment in any of them than

> "Pinnacled, solitary, I can find
> your face, but not your eon: could you burn
> across my calendar that none has read,"
>   etc.

I hope you got the copy of *The Bare Hills* I forwarded to you from the publisher. I'll expect the books you mentioned today or tomorrow. I'm keen about reading Hopkins so do, please, send him. And your thought about sending other books from the library is kindness itself. I may ask you for something or other soon. This is very hastily written, I hope you will forgive; for we are off for a day at Santa Monica in a few minutes. Please give my sincere regards to Janet Lewis—and try to hope for better from me when I get my head out of the configurations of the *Prophetic Books!*

Hart Crane

2160 Mar Vista
Jan. 20th '28

Dear Winters:
    I can't help rejoicing that someone has come to the rescue of

my Grandmother, for above and beyond the bellowing and wal-
lowing, there was the odiously patronizing reference to one of my
relatives, which I may yet feel justified in answering, albeit it can
only provoke mirth, no matter what *I* may say. The admirable
temper of your letter, however, should prompt me to leave well
enough alone. After all, anyone who reads "My Grandmother's
Love Letters" will notice that Kay Boyle hasn't. . . . But it's really
the spectacle of anyone getting away with such snottiness that gets
my goat. She apparently has no sense of pride or professional
integrity.

I'm glad that Laura likes me and my work, but I hope she
never gets herself (and incidentally me) so wound up in a ball of
yarn. Is she trying to evolve a critical style from Gertrude Stein?
My God, what prose! Honestly, if I am forced to read much more
of that sort of thing I'll go back and join hands with Morley and
Canby. I've got as far as *Trinc* already. Damned if I don't like
that "Ballad of a Strange Thing" more and more. It has an integrity of rhythm which isn't obvious at first. And I like a number of
other things in the book without, however, thoroughly approving
them. Putnam really has just as much to say as MacLeish, perhaps more, but isn't quite so devious in saying it. My favorites
turn out to be just those of everybody else: Memorial Rain, Selene
Afterwards, Nocturne, Signature for Tempo (1), and Immortal
Helix. That Fragment in *The Caravan* was the best yet. Certainly
MacLeish arouses one's speculations as much as anyone these
days.

The epistemology of the Fernandez book is difficult for me to
grasp. I started the initial chapter several days ago and soon
found myself horribly muddled. I have an idea that he is awfully
long winded and somewhat pretentious — but that is no better
than a prejudice, so far. Meanwhile I shall lay the blame on myself and pray for the advent of a gleam of revelation when I pick
up the book again, which will be soon. Did I shock you once while
you were here by the admission that I had never read *Wuthering
Heights?* Well, I have made up for lost time. Captain Ahab now
has a partner in my gallery of demon-heroes, for I'll not soon forget Heathcliff! You probably read Proust "in the native," but if

you should care to read the translation of *Sodom & Gomorrah* which is just out let me know and I'll send you my copy. The Stanford Library will *not* have that, I feel sure, and as the edition is limited to subscribers you may not find it accessible. I've just about finished it.

I'm sorry I haven't been able to do more justice to the admirable lyrics that you have sent me lately. But as I have more than hinted by numerous actual demonstrations of critical ineptitude lately — I find myself less and less sure of a number of previous persuasions. Finding myself completely disoriented I can hardly pretend to the capacities of a firm judgment on anything but more technical details. And even these are involved in — and justified or disqualified by — the intention or direction of the work as a whole. All this may well be less evolution than involution. But until I get back on the tracks again my word isn't worth much.

Getting back to *transition* — it was a pleasure to see the two Tonita Penas, and "The Fixer" (Hemingway) story was good burlesque. His *Men Without Women* is a book you ought to read. The short story called "The Killers" makes one doff one's hat.

Please remember me to Janet Lewis — and I can't help thanking you for the letter to *transition!*

       Crane

The receipt of Hopkins's poems was important to Crane, and he reacted gratefully. At the same time, his meeting with Winters and the reminder of Winters's continuous productivity urged him toward his own work. Nothing had been accomplished in California except some extended reading that was only incidentally pertinent to his interrupted work on *The Bridge.* "Cape Hatteras," which Winters was to dislike in its finished form, remained a set of incomplete notes. His troubles with his mother were coming to a head, and he was already thinking of leaving Wise. His letters to Winters were cheerful on the surface, and in their correspondence he was notably reticent about the details of his personal and family life, but this letter exhibits a basic uneasiness:

Altadena—
Jan. 27 . 28

Dear Winters:

I hope you are in no great rush for the return of that Hopkins book. It is a revelation to me—of unrealized possibilities. I did not know that words could come so near a transfiguration into pure musical notation—at the same [time] retaining every minute literal signification! What a man—and what daring! It will be long before I shall be quiet about him. I shall make copies of some of the poems, since you say the book is out of print. As yet I haven't come to the theoretical preface—nor Bridges' notes—excepting a superficial glance. Actually—I can't wean my eyes from one poem to go on to the next—hardly—I'm so hypnotized . . .

Having jumped from Proust into *this*—haven't yet got to the Fernandez vol. Nor have I had time to do justice to Janet Lewis' poems—for which, please tell her, I am most thankful—and also for the line drawing—which looks a great deal like you.

I happen to have felt a good deal in one of those parturition times lately—with the clamant [?] hope that I was about to yield "Cape Hatteras" or something equally ambitious at almost any moment . . . but have been so subject to interruptions that I guess the fit has passed off . . . leaving only an irritating collection of notes and phrases defying any semblance of synthesis. I'm going to stop all reading soon in a more-or-less desperate effort to digest and assemble what I've been consuming—or maybe to put it even out of mind. I'd like to get a little work done soon—or else take up copywriting, plastering or plumbing again. . . .

To go back beyond your last—to the mention of Tom Nashe— you named one of my greatest Elizabethan enthusiasms—though all I know of him is his *Unfortunate Traveller*.

Well thanks again to you and Janet Lewis—

Hart Crane

Almost a month intervened before the next letter, so that it opens with apologies. Crane was becoming increasingly bored

with his life as companion to Wise and worried over the condition
of his family. He was a little spiffed when he started the letter,
and he was irritated with Fernandez's *Messages,* for which no sensible person could blame him — it is one dull book. He shared
Winters's annoyance with William Carlos Williams, who singled
out "See Los Angeles First" from the new poems by Winters,
largely, one suspects, because it was close to what Williams himself was working on at the time. And Crane, in his turn, empha-
sizes "The Vigil," probably because it was close to the depressed
and frustrated condition of his own mind.

2160 Mar Vista Ave
Feb 23 '28

Dear Winters:

Since I am becoming chronically remiss in responding to all the
epistolary courtesies of my friends for so long a time past as to be
(or to have been) long since disparaged — I make no more excuses
in detail, beyond the passing recognition of that imperfection, its
millionth confirmation, as it were, with the added addled protest
that I am still, as always, your friend, and that silence is not more
mysterious, in this instance, than (at least) cordial. Further, I
have at present a little Spanish port in my noddle. And who
knows (quien sabe), perhaps the wine is to blame for conceit of
writing you. But enough of bows and furbelows!

Your friend Fernandez — his epistemology and indirections are
on the verge of forcing me to hurl his pretentious tome into the
fire — which is what Wise tells me he did long since, before endur-
ing half so much of his insufferable prose as I have already! I have
to take long vacations and dissipations between glimpses of those
great messages of his, so it is taking me a long time to come to any
decision about him. Meanwhile I'm susceptible to a thousand and
one temptations as momentary reliefs. I am especially consoled
by Wyndham Lewis's latest, *Time and Western Man,* which at
least has a vigorous style, whether or not you agree with all he
says: a bull-headed man, astonishingly sensitive in many ways —
who is a lot better than the usual Doug Fairbanks of controversies.

I advise you to read the book, even though it costs — Well, let me know, and I'll send it to you. . . .

Yes, Williams would naturally prefer such a secondary item as "See L. A. First" to your better things. I've always had my finger on that soft spot in his — no, not brain — but character! He's almost as bad as some of the "revolutionary simpletons" that Lewis lays out, excepting that I'll always concede him a first-rate talent for language. If he'd only let himself alone! He's so afraid he'll find the Zeitgeist at his heels — not realizing that by means of that very attitude it's been *riding* him for some time since.

In "The Vigil" you are at your best, in action, but at something less than that in "registration" . . . I can't help telling you that in such a poem you do not carry me beyond the level of my own station in the laboratory of a like quandary. There is a certain lack of synthesis. I'm in the same fix in regard to my "Cape Hatteras" — a bundle of smoldering notes, no more. I don't know when the proper moment may arrive to grasp them and make them a whole. . . . It's a damned hard time we live in. And I think you stand a much better chance of biding your time beyond it than I do — for a number of reasons.

Glad you liked the Blake. It really IS worth having. I am still discovering new marvels in Hopkins. Do, please, forgive me for withholding these books so long. I'll return them soon. My heartiest greetings to Janet Lewis. . . .

as ever,
Crane

The note of March 7 is little more than a note, and it does not mention any cause for Crane's state of mind. But he had made his decision to quit Altadena, and returning books to Winters was part of the process of clearing out:

2160 Mar Vista Avenue
Altadena, California
March 7th

Dear Winters:

I hope you got the books all right — if not please let me know at once, as I sent them about ten days ago. My letter probably peeved you — in which case I'm sorry. I won't plead excuses however — beyond the fact that I am in a rather unpleasant state of mind all round these days — and am therefore poor company.

I hope that all is well with you. And let me repeat my thanks for your many courtesies.

Yrs.

Crane

Crane moved in with his family, and Winters, on hearing of the ill health and other difficulties of Kay Boyle, decided not to send his letter of protest to *transition*. Winters's *The Bare Hills* had finally appeared from the Four Seas Company, and it had been reviewed by Agnes Lee Freer in *Poetry* and by Allen Tate in *The New Republic*. Agnes Freer took the book with deep seriousness:

Strong winds blow through *The Bare Hills,* a book inspiring in its absolute originality. To some readers, it will signify mere austerity. Others will find tenderness, as they find in it the gigantic conflict of the first movement of Beethoven's *Ninth Symphony,* or in the fateful tones of Brahms' *Tragic Overture.* Important and remarkable, it may be better understood in France than in America, for Frenchmen are not afraid of the dark. Yvor Winters cannot complain if, after some of the sophisticated cadences of today have died out, Time, the flow of which is almost a physical sensation of pain to him, but Time in the only conception the average person has of it, brings these sculptured poems to a place in what men call the future.[8]

And Allen Tate, describing how the book goes "Beyond Imagism," found in it "a classical precision of statement, a kind of naked elegance, which no other contemporary poet commands."[9]

The reference to Benét has to do with one of William Rose Benét's unfortunate attempts at humor, a review of *White Buildings* that degenerates into a set of impertinent parodies.[10]

1803 N. Highland
Hollywood, Calif.
March 29th '28

Dear Winters:

I'm glad you withdrew the protest in *transition* for I don't believe in booting anyone when he's disabled or "down." "Hell of a
world" is right! I feel like an episode from Cervantes since going
to Pedro last Sat. night to meet a friend of mine from the east
who worked his way clear out to see me — as a waiter on a steamer.
Five thugs waylaid us, beat us nearly insensible and robbed us of
everything. I finally got him back to his bunk — but am still worried sick about his condition. The ship left next morning without
my being able to get aboard to see him.

I haven't yet seen the *Poetry* review, but whatever objections I
might have felt are already obviated. The Benet jibe has also
escaped me — unless it is the mention of "The Tunnel," which
dates back to January or earlier. I'm piqued by curiosity. Could
you lend me the clipping, if you still have it? You are the best cud-
gel wielder I know, and I'd hate to miss the swing of your blow.

Your second-last letter would have been answered before this if
my affairs had been more settled. I left Mr. Wise's mansion about
a week ago. It was a very distracting place and I regardless, had
come to the unshakable conviction that I was needed elsewhere.
So I am remaining on here — in order to do what I can to alleviate
the predicament of my mother, who is confined every moment by
her attendance on my grandmother. The two are quite alone out
here, and I couldn't go back east with enough mental ease to
make it in any way profitable.

This decision has thrown me into the familiar scrimmage for
employment. I'll secure something in the way of mechanical writing — advertising or scenario — with one of the movie companies if
possible. Not that I prefer it to some other jobs, but I must secure
the maximum cash to in any way fulfil my purpose in staying. My
own projects in any case, will have to go hang, at least for awhile.
But I hope I shall have sparks left over to redeem the waste of
time that bread and butter claims.

Tate's review was well written, and to me seemed very laudatory. I know it to have been completely sincere. In a way it was more "fortunate" than his preface to my work.

I'm rushing off to an interview — so my mind is too preoccupied to do anything justice at the moment. But I owe you better, and shall try to *do* better in the next few days. Meanwhile, as always, I'm grateful for your patience!

Hastily,
Crane

Winters's review of *Fugitives: An Anthology of Verse,* appeared in *Poetry* in May 1928 and marked a departure for Winters: it was the first time that he reviewed a book of which he did not approve. His sole positive purpose was to talk with general approval of the poems of Allen Tate, and his main negative impulse was to decry the impact of T. S. Eliot on poetic style. The review occasioned a bitter response from John Crowe Ransom and a complaint from Tate. Crane liked it, not only because it attacked Eliot, whose *The Waste Land* he was attempting to counteract in *The Bridge,* but also because Winters recommended Crane — along with Baudelaire, Corbière, Hardy, Dickinson, and Hopkins — as a proper guide for young Americans who wished to achieve anything poetically. They should look to "the spiritual *and* formal values of two poets — Hart Crane, and especially that of the most magnificent master of English and of human emotions since Thomas Hardy, William Carlos Williams."[11]

May 7th '28

Dear Winters:

Your review of *The Fugitives* is full of nails well hit and powerfully driven. And you manage to cover an amazing amount of ground! You can't imagine how much such writing means to me these days of fad and insipid compromises. It is evident that you are not reserving your onslaught against Eliot for your book of criticism announced for next year! And you are dead right in at-

tacking Eliot's followers in manner and attitude. When you come
to a man like MacLeish, though, I think you may find him harder
to dispose of creatively than Eliot himself. He is really illusive —
perhaps not genuinely anything — as he has displayed himself in
several successive postures.... Anyway, I like your good solid
opinions. It takes a stoic to have them nowadays.

The Benet jibes were all too obvious to do much more than
point back to the idiotic mind that dared boast of such stubborn
density. The Canby Crap Can is always full of such complacen-
cies. I'd rather prompt their ridicule than their praise.

Isidor Schneider recently sent me his new poems — and wondered if you'd like a copy. I said yes. *Anthony* has vigor and confusion and a lot of other features — nearly everything but major
form. But I like a few of the shorter poems — *Sunday Morning,
Funeral, Whatever you seek,* etc. None of them flash or sing however as even the second-best of Williams — but Schneider's drol-
lery is good even if heavy, — in places.

I see you have read *Wuthering Hts.* But the one apparent va-
gary in your review seems to me your mention of that book in connection with Racine. It ought either to have been amplified or
omitted. At least I can't relate it in any definite way to the "inadequacy of former spankings." I haven't read much by Herbert —
just neglect, not lack of interest. Marvell is another that I didn't
encounter until lately. Do you know the wonderful lines (57-66)
in his *The First Anniversary* — where the building of Thebes is
described? They have that perfection of solidity and inward
movement so hard to equal in any modern forms.

Any chance of our meeting here this summer?

Yrs.

Hart Crane

There was no chance of their meeting again that summer, or
ever again. On June 27, Crane would write to Winters from Patterson in a happy vein and with only a brief explanation of his
precipitous departure from Hollywood.

VII

THE LAST PHASE

After Crane left California, the correspondence with Winters did not deteriorate — it simply dwinded away. Crane was preoccupied with his family and economic problems, which were inseparable. Leaving his mother and grandmother in Hollywood was an act of flight that he sustained for the rest of his life. He was never to see his mother again, and his grandmother died in September. From his arrival in Patterson until his departure for Europe in December, there was very little calm in his life. Now that he was famous and his work sought after by magazines, he had nothing to send; no progress was made on *The Bridge,* and after some spectacular misconduct, even Mrs. Turner could not put up with him any longer. He was cast adrift and wandered from friend to friend, getting temporary jobs in an advertising company and in a bookstore. His friends were loyal, but his depression was generally constant. Writing to Winters would remind him of his wasted poetic vocation, and that was too painful to contemplate.

His letter written shortly after arriving in Patterson is jovial enough, partly because of sustaining memories of the Mississippi and New Orleans, and more surely because of his sense of release from the clutching troubles of his mother. Winters was deep in the study of renaissance poetry and offered his reading list and if necessary copies of texts. Crane's response was friendly but not encouraging.

Patterson, New York
June 27th, 1928

Dear Winters:

I left the Coast on the 15th of last month. I had thought that I had given the hasty signal of at least a postcard dropped off the station platform at Houston or San Antonio, but evidently not, judging by your good letter received this morning via Hollywood. I left in a hurry, but not without due deliberation. You already know my grudges against the L.A. population, but perhaps you don't know my full distaste for family turmoils. At any rate ... here I am again in the old house with the old woman and her cats, and sneezing as strenuously as ever at the date of roses ... and damned good and glad to rejoin a few human associates who live around here and to smell a little horse manure again.

The boat ride down the Mississippi to the Gulf was, of course, something of a heart-throb to me. One day only is enough to make one sentimental about New Orleans. I never before felt so in the presence of the "old" America — not baldly "confronted" with it, as at places like Salem, Mass. — but surrounded and rather permeated by it. But I suppose pewter is the more representative, and the old tarnished gold of Orleans belongs rather to the traditions of Martinique than to the spirit of the Minute Men. I'd like to spend a winter there sometime, anyway. And the Mississippi delta is all that I ever dreamed it to be. Then I had four more days on the water before a sight of land. It's just as cheap as the northern routes, and to me a lot less tiresome, though longer.

Nathan Asch and his wife as well as the Cowleys and Josephsons are close neighbors of mine this summer. There is also a cashiered army officer turned bootlegger over on Birch Hill, who makes very good applejack. But in spite of all this whirl, not to mention the usual croquet tournaments up at Slater Brown's place, I intend to get something done before going into N.Y. later for a job. I've met Williams before, but I'm hoping to know him better when he comes out here soon as a guest of the Asches. They are also hoping to get Morley Callaghan down from Canada for a brief spell ... but I'm beginning to sound like a maitre d'hotel.

To get back in the files a little — I am glad that my dear old Kit still gives you so much kick. I am always amazed at the glorious cornucopia that Tamburlaine shakes page after page. I enjoy the antiquated spelling even in this case, of the Oxford edition, wherein the buskins of Hero are described as a "woonder to behold." Truly, the very prologue to Tamburlaine and the very first words set the key for the diviniest human feasting:

> *From iygging vaines of riming mother wits,*
> *And such conceits as clownage keeps in pay...*

What a "flourish without" to signal the whole Age of Elizabeth! and a promise that was truly kept! I have been haunted by those two lines so many times, and always wonder in what consists their strange combination of tangibility and illusions. You get it also in Keats's "Eve of St. Agnes," but not in quite so joyous, so robust a form. The very kindly jaggedness of the Marlowe lines endears them more, at least at times, than the suave perfections that somehow reached a little over the line, into death, with Keats.

The tremendous lines from Blake that you wanted are on page *763.* They always strike me as about the most final lines ever written. At your mention of Traherne I have been looking over some specimens in an anthology I have and can't imagine why once, years ago, I failed to appreciate his astonishing validity. Vaughan, whom he certainly bears a likeness to, really does bore me excepting a handful of complete poems and scattered lines in others. It lies rather with a kind of Presbyterianism that infects Vaughan, I surmise; whereas Traherne's piety is more universalized, more positive. You even begin to suspect him of apocalyptic casuistry here and there, so crystalline and capable is his bended head, when lo! by adding even more wit to the occasion he convinces you of his complete absence of vanity. Almost a Brahmin in some ways.

I'll follow your advice and read more of Herbert. Cowley has a copy down the road. But please don't bother about the proferred copy of Traherne — not that I wouldn't love to have it, but I'm so near N.Y. now, that such books are once more accessible. You may be interested in watching for some forthcoming articles in the *Outlook:* Cowley on Poe; Tate on Emily; Burke on Emerson (I think), etc. I haven't been able to get advance carbons from any of them, but these three generally have something worthy of interest. Cowley has a rather slow, laborious mind that simply cannot turn out a shoddy sentence. I would rather talk to him about the sheer mechanics of poetry than anyone I know—that is since Tate has become too pontifical for any discussions whatever. Which reminds me of the protests you mention receiving for your Fugitive review. I suspect you irritated a great deal by spelling his first name All*a*n instead of All*e*n. He raised such a row with Liveright about that misdemeanor on the title page of *White Bldgs.* that the whole edition was torn up, new title pages inserted and rebound. As to the locutions of Marianne—she seems to have had at least a good time with her briefer on your book. I shall never be able to make out the meaning of "apperceptions . . . whose cumulative eloquence recedes in geometrical inverse ratio to imperativeness." For God's sake, somebody play the "Kitten on the Keys," PLEASE! All this exudes a "flabby algebraic odor"— which in one of Cummings' poems is descriptive of a good-sized c—t.

I didn't mean to end matters so oderiferously; I'm sure I can congratulate you on your pups, anyway, if not on your Turgid Mention.

> *All best,*
> *Crane*

On July 31, Winters wrote to Harriet Monroe about her reaction to Crane's "Moment Fugue," after Crane had sent him her note on the poem. Winters probably destroyed Monroe's note, as he destroyed practically all his correspondence, but his letter to her is preserved in the Poetry Magazine Papers at the University of Chicago Library. It is not quite so amusing as Crane and his friends found it. Winters made a reasonable paraphrase of the poem and managed to offend the staff of *Poetry* in the process.

His letter elicited an acerbic note from Jessica North, who had been responsible for the initial note to Crane. And Winters wrote a scathing reply. *Poetry* did not publish the poem.

New York City
Aug. 17th, 1928

Dear Winters:

Aunt Harriet deserved the justling. Cowley and some others have had a good time reading the carbon you sent, which you don't mind my having shown, I hope. . . .

I'm in the big, simmering gluepot Metropolis hunting work. Not much to say in any direction and slightly dizzy.

So you'll forgive my brevity, I hope. I'd give you my present address, but it's so uncertain for any length of time that you'd better keep me at Patterson, whence forwarding is more certain.

As ever,
Hart Crane

Three weeks later Crane had found a job and a remedy for hay fever, but he could not forget the effrontery of Jessica North's joking (as she saw it) attempts to diagram the sentences of "Moment Fugue" and failing. Crane was too troubled to write a proper letter. His grandmother had died on September 6, bringing sorrow and new troubles.

77 Willow St
Brooklyn, N. Y.
Sept. 9th '28

Dear Winters:

I'm back again where I can see the harbor from my window, and Brooklyn Bridge. Also I've found a job (copywriting) as well as a remedy for hay fever that really seems to work. In regard to the last, if you have any other sneezing critters among your friends who need relief remember to tell them of the following two remedies which team beautifully — Rinex (internally) and *Estivin* (for eyes). More violent cases should apply to Miss Jessicum North, Mother Superior of Thunder Mug University, Illinois, for summary advice and parsing treatment. . . .

Have been reading Laura Riding's "Contemporaries and Snobs" (Jonathan Cape) and recommend parts of the first 100 pages as some really remarkable analysis, fumblingly expressed, but damned suggestive. *And* have you heard Bach's *Toccata & Fugue in D Minor* on the Orthophonic yet? The Philadelphia Symphony gives it wonderful volume. The pattern and purity of it are beyond praise. The sublimest rhetoric I have ever heard!

My mind is mostly a flat blank these days, that is — what is left of it after it has been crammed and unloaded several times every day, the material being CALOROIL HEATERS, FOS-FOR-US MINERAL MIXTURE (for hogs, cattle, poultry) and FLOWER OF LOVE WEDDING RINGS, etc. etc. The high tension rush of an agency office is only to be compared with a newspaper office. Inserts, folders, circulars, posters, full pages and half pages, a two-column twenty-liner here, there this there that! But I'm not sorry to be working and, in fact, was damned lucky to get anything as good right now.

When I get a little back on my feet financially I'll feel a little more like a man. Meanwhile you seem to have the gracious facility of making me believe that I am possibly at least a poet.

> *All best, hastily,*
> Hart Crane

Winters was troubled by the letter and the previous silence. He was at the time busy contemplating Allen Tate's *Mr. Pope and Other Poems* and preparing a review for the *New Republic*. He wrote extensively to Tate, praising his work and finding in it the only major poetry by a contemporary other than Crane. Shortly after receiving Crane's letter he wrote on September 15 to Tate, acting as a conciliator between the two men, having found Crane's isolation and unhappiness painful. He asked Tate not to be irritated by Crane, who had told him at their meeting in California that Tate was annoyed with him. Winters conceded that Crane might be hard to take in personal association but because of the quality of his mind and work, he was one of very few people who should be accepted and tolerated, whatever just occasion for irritation his disorderly conduct might create. Tate found the moral advice impertinent, and he did not write to Winters again until December when he was on his way to Europe. Winters's assurance that Crane admired Tate immensely did not move him. Crane in this difficult period of his life had become a trial to his friends. Tate's patience and generosity had been called on too often, and Winters had seen Crane only at his most engaging and sober moments.

After his grandmother's death, Crane's troubles with his mother increased. She refused to sign the papers that would permit him to receive his legacy from his grandmother's estate, and she kept urging him to join her in California. That was the last intent in Crane's mind; his main desire was to keep as far from his mother as possible, and he intended to use his share of his grandmother's estate to keep, as Unterecker puts it, not only a continent between them but an ocean as well. Europe was his destination. With all his confusing and embittering problems, attention to purely literary matters was impossible, so that some six weeks lapsed before he wrote again to Winters. The occasion was Winters's review of Tate, appearing in the *New Republic* for October 17.

110 Columbia Heights
Brooklyn, N. Y.
Oct. 23 '28

Dear Winters:

I won't enumerate all the excuses I've had for my negligence of you. They wouldn't seem valid to you without inexcusable details

on my part, and perhaps even then you'd need a slice of Baby-
lonian routine yourself, directly experienced, before you'd be
able to summon the necessary charity.

I've started two or three letters, been interrupted or obliged to
complete some office work at home, etc. etc. But I have wanted
to say something about the three sonnets you sent, long before
this, and even now they aren't with me. So I can only give you my
preferences: the Emily one first, the one ending — "I'm dead, I'm
dead" next. But the other one, though ambitious and solid emotionally, somehow falls short of a sufficiently rich intonation.
Allen Tate is more successful sometimes at expressing something
of the same feeling of cerebral thunder in a vacuum, "invisible
lyric seeds the mind," etc. But I think this group is superior, less
strained than the sonnets in the Caravan.

Your review of Tate in the N.R. strikes me as nothing less than
noble. Of course I resent being posed in a kind of All American
Lyric Sprint with anyone, as the competitive idea seems foreign to
my idea of creation. But that is probably too personal a reaction
to have any pertinence to the major critical issues of the review. I
also think that while Tate has a very complex mind and possibly a
wider grasp of ideas than I do — he nevertheless has not come to
any closer grips with his world than to simply state the dilemma
in a highly inferential manner, which we're all obliged to do most
of the time. Tate's greatest rage against me at times has been on
account of my avowed (and defended) effort to transcend these
Eliotish sighs and tribulations, and to reach some kind of positive
synthesis.

Tate faces the issue more squarely than the later Eliot. I like
your appreciation of his really unflinching valor. But when you
speak of my "illusions" you convince me that you surely are mis-
taken in a number of my intentions. I am not content with being
an absolute Stoic. I mean, stoicism isn't my goal, even though I'm
convinced as much as you and Tate are, of the essentially tragic
background of existence. There's something entirely too passive
about stopping there (I don't care if even so great a poet as Hardy
did!) and counting out, like the beating of a clock, the "precon-

ceived" details of disappointment. For that is the stoic's pride—
that all will pass but his endurance. It seems to me that Aeschylus, assuming the same materials, does a lot more with them. At
least he makes something out of them, call it all illusion or not.

After many inquiries and some intrigue, even, I'm back in the
old house where I have a view of the harbor again. Rooming
houses depress me terribly, and this is about the only one that sets
me reading and writing a little, though I actually haven't had
time, with the rush at the office, to read more than the usual reviews on the can or in the subway. I suspect I'll soon be off your
list if I don't do better.

> *Yours,*
> *Crane*

This was to be the last substantial letter in their correspondence for more than a year. One short letter refers briefly to the
problems with his mother and gives a forwarding address in London.

> *110 Columbia Heights*
> *Brooklyn, N. Y.*
> *Nov. 29th, '28*

Dear Winters:

I've been encircled too much by the whirlwind hysterics of—
well, Fate (if one may allude to one's family in that way) to
answer your last. And it isn't possible now, either.

I am hoping to get off to London on the 8th of next month, if
the feat can be managed. May stay in Europe a couple of years,
some quiet and secluded working hours on the island of Majorca
being my objective.

At any rate, the best address I can give for the next month is
c/o The Guaranty Trust Co., 50 Pall Mall. S. W. 1, London. I'm

sorry to be so limited right now in my responses, but it may be that distance will lend me a part of my thinking and speaking apparatus again.

> *Best wishes, as ever,*
> *Hart Crane*

A final postcard promises letters after arrival in London.

Am on my way as per schedule. I'll be able to write after I get to London — or later on the way. Please excuse delay.

> *Hart*

The letters would not be forthcoming, so that from the period between December of 1928 and December of 1929, the relations between the two men broke off, not because of any dispute or rancor but because of Crane's reluctance to continue the kind of serious literary discussions and considerations that mark his correspondence with Winters. The correspondence might have become less sympathetic, for Winters was consolidating his sense of poetics and establishing new directions for his work and thought. In his freshly developed optique, his admiration for Crane's work diminished, so that Crane became the object of probing analytical judgment rather than the occasion for appreciative reviews, essays, and letters.

The silence that fell over the correspondence of Crane and Winters between December 1928 and January 1930 was matched, in Crane's career, by a year of relative public silence. During 1929 Crane published in magazines only three poems, two of them written much earlier, the third — "A Name for All" — a poem so dull that it is hard to believe Crane could have written it and astonishing that he should have published it. It almost seems that

he had ceased to take poetry seriously, and if it had not been for
the enthusiasm of Harry and Caresse Crosby, he would quite
probably never have written the three sections of *The Bridge*—
"Indiana," "Cape Hatteras," "Quaker Hill"—that marked his
only significant productivity after the completion of "The River."
And those three sections have been seriously questioned by the
bulk of students of Crane's work; they are among the weakest segments of the poem. The Crosbys were so taken by the work completed before Crane's arrival in Paris in January of 1929 that they
did not feel it necessary for Crane to write any more of the poem.
Crane still felt committed to the design that he had described to
Otto Kahn, Winters, and others, and one of the terrible agonies
he underwent during that period grew from his dissatisfaction
with his new work and the doubts this cast on the entire project.
The excitement of life in Paris was no compensation for the frus-
trations that overwhelmed him as he contemplated the ruins of
his poetic enterprise. Solitude in southwest France and a visit to
Robert Graves in the Camargue were no help, and dissipation in
Marseilles gave temporary satisfaction but left him with his overwhelming problem. In addition to his troubles with his writing,
and growing from them, his sexual excesses became more fla-
grant, his drinking uncontrollable, and his violence so spectacular that his brawling in the Café Select led to arrest, imprison-
ment, a brutal beating by the police, a fine, and a very stern
judicial warning.

He managed to get some work done on "Cape Hatteras" in
France, but when he left for the United States in July, the months
in Europe had been largely wasteful. Two years had passed since
the brief period of happiness and productivity that resulted in
"The River." His morale was destroyed, and as his drinking continued he was afflicted with hallucinations and nightmares. Only
the loyalty of a few friends remained and helped him to do what
he could on *The Bridge,* until in December he gave the poem
over to the Crosbys for publication by the Black Sun Press. He
had concluded, as best he could, the labor of years. On December 26 he sent the final revised version of "Quaker Hill" to Caresse

Crosby with a postscript asking her to send a review copy to Yvor
Winters.[1] So that year ended, with the suicide of Harry Crosby,
the unsatisfactory completion of his ambitious project, and pros-
pects that were unclear.

For Winters the year had been very different. While Crane was
living an extreme version of the image of the bohemian poet,
Winters was living a quiet and productive life as a happily married literary student, with the satisfactions of a rural setting and
the pleasures of systematic academic study. Poetry continued to
come, though in traditional measures rather than free verse, and
under the tutelage of William Dinsmore Briggs and in company
with new and admiring friends, neighbors, and fellow graduate
students he explored the range of verse in English from Chaucer
on, while maintaining and extending his interest in French verse
from Baudelaire through Valéry. He also began writing his first
extended critical prose since his master's thesis at Colorado in
1925, in preparation for his doctoral dissertation and to define
his own poetics. That enterprise began in 1928, and by August 20
of that year, he had completed the important and incisive essay
that formulated the intent and design of his doctoral thesis and
his eventual first critical book, *Primitivism and Decadence*. The
essay was published in *American Caravan* for 1929 under the title
"The Extension and Reintegration of the Human Spirit, Through
the Poetry Mainly French and American Since Poe and Baudelaire."[2] He continued shuffling the poems in *Fire Sequence* and
adding new poems. Early in 1929 he began publishing in mimeographed form *The Gyroscope,* including new work by himself and
others and severe commentaries on current literary practice.
Winters was active in all aspects of the poetic enterprise. He went
on writing brief reviews and fresh poems as well as his extensive
critical work and his editing. He was busy, happy, and productive. He continued raising Airedales, and at the instigation of
Janet Lewis Winters — who was tired of making drawings of dogs
— acquired goats and other animals. They maintained an extensive vegetable garden that would ease the economic troubles of life
during the Great Depression. The antithesis to Crane is striking.

At this point the two men seem to be living out the allegorical types with which they have been associated, antithetical in social and inner life. Winters profited from his stability by maintaining a continuous flow of verse and criticism, and he also used his relative freedom to articulate the basis of his thought about life and art. In the academic year 1928-29, he was supported by his father, so that his life was set in a frugal design but he was free of the interruptions of teaching. What emerged from his investigations and meditations was the rational stoicism that would mark his basic point of view from that time onward. It had always been in the background of his thought; now it became systematic and primary. Basically, Winters accepted the view of science that dominated Hardy's thought and was evident in coarser terms in Jacques Loeb. The escape to mysticism, which he associated with Crane, he found evasive and untrue. When Yeats's *The Tower* appeared in 1928 he thought it the only Yeats that was genuinely major, but he despised what he took to be the charlatanry of "The Gift of Harun Al-Rashid." His dislike of mysticism and especially of spiritualism came from his childhood experience. His mother correctly predicted the death of some twenty people, and when he was very young dragged him off to séances; his reaction drove him to his youthful interest in the sciences, and it was one of the formative forces in his life. His experience in the tuberculosis sanatorium reinforced his inclination toward stoicism.

I do not mean that Winters in his later work accepted completely and without qualification the mechanistic structure of the world. His sonnet "The Invaders" is eloquent testimony to the limits of the scientific view, but it is ambivalent. What the invaders have done is, in a phrase that echoes through his thought, to strip life bare, and in the process to dissolve "our heritage of earth and air!" The color of the earth has been stripped, leaving "The naked passion of the human mind." This mental passion is demonic, and as Grosvenor E. Powell has argued, Winters took the concept of the demon very seriously:

> Aquinas tells us that a demon may be said to be good in so far as he may be said to exist; that he is a demon in so far as his existence is incomplete. This statement is a necessary part

of the doctrine of evil as deprivation. But a demon, or a genius, may be almost wholly deprived of being in large areas in which theoretically he ought to exist, and at the same time may have achieved an extraordinary degree of actuality in the regions in which he does exist; and when this happens, his persuasive power, his possessive power, is enormous, and if we fail to understand his limitations he is one of the most dangerous forces in the universe. Our only protection against him is the critical faculty, of which, I fear, we have far too little.[3]

What matters in the scientific view of the universe is its "extraordinary degree of actuality," and its incompleteness is one compelling argument for the imaginative force of art, which can restore to experience those qualities that the demon of "The naked passion of the human mind" cannot realize or entertain. In the period from 1928 through 1929, Winters developed in the fullest form those ideas that would characterize his mind thenceforward. What was lacking in the modern view of the world was any justification of a moral point of view. The horror of the human condition was so great that only the great artist could face and control it:

> The facts of life at best are disheartening; the vision of life which man has little by little constructed (or perhaps one should say stripped bare) is all but crushing. . . . The artist who is actually ignorant of the metaphysical horror of modern thought or who cannot feel it imaginatively — and there are many such — is of only a limited, a more or less decorative, value. But the artist who can feel the full horror, organize it into a dynamic attitude or state of mind, asserting by that very act his own life and the strength and value of his own life, and who can leave that state of mind completed behind him for others to enter, has performed the greatest spiritual service that can be performed.[4]

In contrast with this noble stance, Winters derided the mystic and the nihilist for their evasions and their lack of courage. He never explicitly defines the "metaphysical horror of modern thought," though he seems at one point to identify it with a "sense of time in an incomprehensible universe." The horror is also associated with that solipsistic mysticism that Winters was convinced led to self-annihilation. Mysticism, nihilism, or the scientific view "stripped bare" by years of study and experiment — these alternatives were inferior to what should best be called a kind of "moral aestheticism." Winters writes that

> Art is the most intense moment of consciousness: the intensity of the moment of fusion is the final moral assertion of the artist, who by that act *makes an integral part of his own dynamic existence* the fact that he has met [life], no matter how terrible it may be. It is the final proof that he, as a self-directed integer, is morally superior to the facts of life. A successful poem, then, may be, as an experience and a moral evaluation, a negation of the ideational material that it contains. This fact alone can explain the spiritual security to be found in the most terrible of the tragic poets.[5]

This passage presents certain difficulties, though I am at a loss to think of a way that the difficulties could be avoided. Art differs from experience; the moment of fusion is the total imaginative and moral understanding of the data of experience and is not to be confused with mere intensity of emotion or perception. Unlike the metaphysical pantheist, the artist is superior to the aggregate of data; unlike the nihilist, he asserts as a high value his own capacity to achieve through his dynamic existence a moral superiority to meaningless data; unlike the scientist he creates a moral and aesthetic entity that transcends the merely mechanistic and abstract. Art thus becomes the basis rather than the expression of meaningful experience. Winters makes the highest possible claim for the importance of art, but he cannot demonstrate its legitimacy; he makes an assertion, an act of faith.

And that is what the preliminary sections of the essay on "The Extension and Reintegration of the Human Spirit" compose, an assertion of passionate belief. With variations and extensions, it would remain the center of Winters's thought about art and letters.

The remainder of the essay goes over ground that Winters

would cover more fully in *Primitivism and Decadence,* notably
his taxonomy of poetic methods, and material discussed in earlier
work on Imagism and in his correspondence with Crane and
Tate. Winters continues to treat Crane's work with great respect,
and he adduces him as an example of a poet whose verse em-
bodies a fusion of allegorical with imagistic qualities:

> Such things as *Serenade at the Villa,* for instance, or most
> of Hart Crane, implicate entire ranges of ideation and feel-
> ing that cannot be reduced to any formula save the poem
> itself.... Hart Crane, by means of his semi-allegorical
> method, continually and most often successfully attempts to
> evade an unequivocal statement...by constantly running
> his allegory ashore on the specific. He is an example of a soul
> with a natural taste for the schematized and abstract being
> forced by his milieu toward the specific; and it is on the spe-
> cific that by far the greater part of the important poetry of
> the last eighty years has been based in the main.[6]

Crane's merits are illustrated by comments on "Repose of Rivers":

> We have here an obvious and commonplace symbol—the
> course of a river standing for the life of man—and the mono-
> logue is presumably spoken by the river itself. The symbolic
> value of the details, however, is not so precisely determinable
> —they are details not of the life of man nor even directly re-
> ferable to the life of man, but are living and marvelous de-
> tails of a river's course, with strange intellectual and emo-
> tional overtones of their own. Mr. Robert Penn Warren has
> remarked that the life of an allegorical poem resides pre-
> cisely in that margin of meaning that cannot be interpreted
> allegorically....the words are constantly balancing on, al-
> most slipping from, the outermost edge of their possible
> meaning. Their meaning is defined frequently not by the
> dictionary, but by their relation to other words about them
> in the same predicament.[7]

Crane read the essay and was pleased by it; it was one of the few
critical works that he read seriously during 1929. The sympathetic

treatment of his poetry he appreciated and had come to expect. Winters was placing him in the company of Baudelaire and Mallarmé, and in his conclusion described Crane's poetry as among the major efforts and great achievements of the century.

After the break in his correspondence with Crane, Winters continued writing to Tate. His interests in traditional form increased, and his respect for Tate's verse mounted. He preferred Tate's new work to Crane's and saw Tate as Baudelaire to Crane's Rimbaud. In a long letter written on Christmas night of 1928, on the verge of Tate's departure for Europe, he apologized for having tried to intervene in Tate's relation with Crane, expressing his continued regrets that the two most intelligent men in New York should have quarreled. Under the tutelage of William Dinsmore Briggs he read Thomas Aquinas and widened and deepened his knowledge of the traditions of English poetry, comparing the cadences of Crashaw with the definitions of Aquinas. After Tate's arrival in Europe, Winters maintained the correspondence. His opinions had not yet settled, and when he reread Emerson he compared him favorably with Valéry and set him a little lower than Dickinson. Tate received a copy of *The Gyroscope,* and as the year progressed Winters found more and more merit in Tate's new verse, suggesting that only the late work of Hardy was better. He continued writing sonnets and experimented with heroic couplets. He sought in his own work and found in Tate's the intellectual discipline and definition that he believed to be the only true bases for meaningful development.

The essays that Winters wrote for *The Gyroscope* established a tone and point of view that were austere and in Winters's sense of the term classical. Crane could not have read them carefully; otherwise he would not have been surprised at Winters's review of *The Bridge.* In his "Statement of Purpose" for the magazine, Winters specifically opposed "all doctrines of liberation and emotional expansionism" and "religious expansionism," including all forms of mysticism. He opposed all "doctrines which advocate that the poet 'express' his country (Whitmanian Rousseauism) or his time."[8] He had other animadversions, but these would be enough to condemn Crane's effort. In the third issue of *The Gyro-*

scope, Winters made some notes on contemporary criticism that reveal some of the arbitrary dogmatism that is familiar to readers of his later work. The occasion for the notes are essays by Tate and Eliot that Winters interprets as asserting that there is no adequate rational basis for ethics. Eliot's famous essay in his homage to Lancelot Andrewes announced his embracing of the Anglican faith; Tate's essay on the fallacy of Humanism left him, as Winters saw the matter, in a very ambiguous position. Winters scorns ambiguities, and he needs no basis for an ethical position — without faith and revelation, and modern man cannot accept either, the best choice is simply the least comforting of the various ethical possibilities. The source of evil is in emotion, and the reduction of emotion to a minimum is the only way to a controlled and harmonious life. As far as belief is concerned, the only necessity is a belief in existence. The ideal point of view is that of the disinterested observer.

Winters seems in this essay to go beyond stoicism to a kind of emotional masochism, but he thought of himself as redressing a balance. To his mind the Stoics failed because they refused to take the emotions into account at all and looked to a pure order of the intellect. He was willing to admit what he called the "irreducible emotion" and thought that emotion so revealed by disciplined moral evaluation might then be a source of good rather than evil. Such an emotion would be the substance of a work of art. Unlike the Stoic collapse, the modern point of view originated in "an orgy of emotionalism (over a century long) at the expense of intellect." Aristotle, he conceded, saw the feelings rather than reason as "the principle of and guide to virtue," but he affirms that Aristotle

> provides the feelings, however, with a very powerful intellectual substructure and a profoundly difficult emotional discipline, of which the arts are an important part. These notes, then, are basically Aristotelian.[9]

As so often with the criticism of the later Winters, one has to look beyond the dogmatic assertion to the motive force. The main motive is isolating and purifying the fundamental nature of art and, more specifically, poetry. He would take a man's poetry as a better guide to his ethics than any purely ethical statement. The notes were extensions of earlier work, and what is new in them is the brusqueness and bluntness of their tone.

Crane could not have read carefully Winters's essays written during the break in their correspondence, though he laid claim to having at least seen them. Over a year since his departure for Europe, he sent Winters a carbon copy of *The Bridge* in its final form, assuming that Winters would be willing to write a review. He had already asked Caresse Crosby to send a copy of the final printed version to Winters for that purpose. The letter is a curious one; after all, the two men had written steadily to each other for more than two years, and forty-four of Crane's communications are extant, only to have the correspondence broken without explanation. Crane is reasonable to assume that Winters would take the resumption of the relationship with some surprise, but he is truthful when he asserts that he had written to very few people, and then briefly, during the period. The letter is candid, and it is a saddening revelation of Crane's insecurity with his work which simply would not permit the intrusion of another sensibility that could increase his doubts and worries. He might have profited from the criticism, but it would certainly have slowed him down, and that was the last thing he wanted.

> 190 Columbia Heights
> Brooklyn, N. Y.
> January 14th, 1930

Dear Winters:

In this same mail I'm sending a complete copy of the Bridge — as it is being set up for the Black Sun Edition in Paris now. This edition will be ready about a month from now, the Liveright edition on April 1st.

"A fine time to be writing me!" — you may rightfully observe. But I am hoping that you haven't totally misunderstood my lengthy silence. To begin with, I haven't been in a mood for any sort of correspondence with anyone for a considerable time; and secondly, though you may not consider the statement as complimentary to your power as I do, — I have not wanted, for the time being, to engage myself in any further controversies, metrical, theoretical, ethical or what not, which letters (especially from you) frequently occasion. That kind of stimulus is apt to be dangerous at the time when one is desperately trying to complete any preconceived conception like my Bridge project. But here it is, now — very much larger than I had originally planned it, and at long last, something of a satisfaction, at least to me.

I have asked Mrs. Crosby to send you a copy of the Paris edition for review — not that you actually need review it, but that I want you to have a copy of what is physically one of the most beautiful libros I know of. You ought especially to appreciate the three photographs therein, taken by Walker Evans, a young fellow here in Brooklyn who is doing amazing things.

There is much on which to congratulate you, — especially the superb essay in the Caravan. I have seen a couple of issues of the Gyroscope which were certainly not to be sneezed at. You may put me down as one of your subscribers — with as many of the earlier issues as are available. Also I hope I may hear from you sometime soon, however little I may deserve to.

> Best wishes, as always,
> Hart Crane

Winters replied that he would review *The Bridge,* and Crane was delighted. Reviews from Tate, Cowley, Schneider, and Winters would assure a good press, and he assumed that Winters would use his contacts at *Poetry* to place the review. Their relationship was reestablishing itself at the old comradely level, or so Crane believed.

190 Columbia Heights
January 27th

Dear Winters:

I'm glad to hear that you feel like commenting on the Bridge. Tate has made arrangements to review it for the Hound & Horn, Cowley for the New Republic, and Schneider for the Chicago Eve. Post. I don't know who has taken it for the Herald-Tribune, but out of the list for the Paris edition only two choices remain: Poetry and the Nation.

I recently sent the *Indiana* section to H. M. [Harriet Monroe]. . . . Zabel replied that she was in the east and he was unable to accept it without her consent, however much he wanted to. His attitude was so complimentary and friendly that I judge there may have been some change of mind around their office. At any rate it offers a parallel to their recent invitation to you as described in your letter. I'm glad you're writing for them again. There aren't too many openings for any of us. I'm eager to read your exposé of Jeffers. I've always felt that Jeffers was sincere— but that doesn't quite suffice, —and somewhat "gifted"—to use a horrible word. But everything he has ever written, of any length, at least, excepting The Tower Beyond Tragedy, has given me a vague nausea. He really is a highstepping hysteric, I'm afraid.

You couldn't be expected to like Crosby's work. I find only a little pure ore here and there. I liked him personally, however, and was very disturbed at his death. . . . But since it is quite probable that he desired it as one more "experiment," I've reserved most of my sympathy for his wife.

Thank you for the promised Gyroscopes, though I'm sorry that there won't be any more. It won considerable and respectful notice, but I imagine took too much of your time.

Isn't there some chance of your coming east this spring?

Yours,
Hart Crane

P.S. —The Paris edition will be about the 1st of March. The Liveright edition will be ready on April 1st. The two might as well be reviewed together. Here are the proper headings for your review: THE BRIDGE. by Hart Crane. Paris. The Black Sun Press. $10.00.

THE BRIDGE. by Hart Crane. New York. Horace Liveright.
$2.50.

Paris edition is limited to 200 copies on Holland Van Gelder, at
$10.00. 50 copies on vellum (autographed) at $25.00. If you
know of anyone interested in getting the Paris edition refer him to
Harry F. Marks, Bookseller, 31 West 47th St. N. Y. who is the
agent here for all Black Sun publications.

Crane might have had some hesitations if he had read Winters's
letter to Tate with serious reservations about the three added sections. Winters wanted time to read and reread the whole before
making up his mind.

Winters did not send an advance copy of the review to Crane,
and the letter previously quoted was the last from Crane which he
preserved. When the review appeared in the June issue of *Poetry,*
Crane was shocked to the point of outrage. The review has excited
a great deal of comment in studies of Crane, most of it sharing
Crane's indignation. Crane wrote Winters a diatribe against it,
and he summarized his arguments in a letter to Isidor Schneider:

> If you have read Winters' attack in the June issue of *Poetry*
> you cannot have been more astonished than I was to note the
> many reversals of opinion he has undergone since reading
> my acknowledgment to Whitman in the later "Cape Hat-
> teras" section.
>
> Had it not been for our previous extended correspondence
> I would not, of course, have written him about it. But as
> things stood I could hardly let silence infer an acceptance on
> my part of all the wilful distortions of meaning, misappropri-
> ations of opinion, pedantry and pretentious classification —
> besides illogic — which his review presents par excellence. I
> must read what prejudices he defends, I understand, against
> writing about subways, in the anti-humanist symposium.
> Poets should defer alluding to the sea, also, I presume, until
> Mr. Winters has got an invitation for a cruise![10]

The review is not one of Winters's best critical commentaries, and it has an unpleasantly pompous tone, particularly in its opening definitions. Crane's disappointment is understandable and justified, especially in view of Winters's encouragement and his high opinion of those segments of *The Bridge* finished by summer of 1928. But the review itself is oddly divided between appreciative comments on lines, passages, and entire sections of the book and a harsh unyielding dislike of the basic motivations. The charges made are the classic ones directed against *The Bridge,* that it lacks structure and coherence, that there is no genuine controlling complex of ideas, that individual sections have limited poetic merit, that although the local texture is often obscure to the point of being impenetrable, only isolated brilliance rescues the book from total failure. From another source, these indictments could have been brushed aside as instances of faulty comprehension and judgment, but Crane prized Winters's opinions and had anticipated a review closer in tone to that of *White Buildings.* Crane's rage came from more than disappointment; Winters was striking at his own feelings of insecurity about the outcome of more than five years of work. In a real sense, Crane's entire career was called into question.

It would have done little good to argue with Winters that *The Bridge* expressed Crane's country, for that was an argument for "Whitmanian Rousseauism," already condemned in his "Statement of Purpose" for *The Gyroscope.* The same statement of principles condemned the attempt of the poet to express his time, all forms of mysticism and religious expansionism, and all doctrines of "liberation and emotional expansionism," anything that subordinated the intellect.[11] Winters's review starts with an attempt to classify *The Bridge,* and he finds it neither epic, didactic, nor a lyric. If anything it is a collection of lyrics in the Whitmanian manner, and that limits the book severely. After a brief outline of the eight sections of the poem, Winters turned to a direct attack on the fallacy of attempting an epic in the Whitmanian manner. The comparison with Vergil shows the limitations of Whitman's point of view, for Vergil had at the background of his work a hierarchy of human values whereas Whitman had no way of discriminating between one type and quality of human experience and another. Hence the Whitmanian tradition permitted either an indiscriminate celebration of energy or, and Winters here cites the example of Jeffers, nihilism. All values being equal, there were none. Whitman, Crane, and Jeffers were capable only of occasional excellences:

> Mr. Crane, since he possesses the greatest genius in the Whitmanian tradition, and since, strangely enough, he grafts onto the Whitmanian tradition something of the stylistic discipline of the Symbolists, most often exceeds himself in this manner.[12]

Winters exemplifies Crane's transcendence of the limits of his tradition by citing the last eight stanzas of "The River" and quoting three, and he so admires the entire passage that he admits "I cannot read it—much less read it aloud—without being profoundly moved."[13]

Winters makes it clear that in pointing out defects in *The Bridge* he is "analyzing the flaws in a genius of a high order."[14] This judgment is crucial to any understanding of Winters's later criticism, of Crane particularly but of Yeats, Frost, Hopkins, and Eliot as well. He took poetry with an abiding seriousness, so that it became a matter of life and death. The more attractive and beguiling the effects of a poet, the more searching the analysis. What troubled Winters as he contemplated the completed form of *The Bridge* was the lack of any "adequate ideational background" in which the perceptions could find something more than the temporary magic of excitement to the point of frenzy.

The brilliance of Crane is not denied in the review, and he concedes that individual lines and passages are superb poetry, that "Cutty Sark" is a perpetual delight, that in fact all the segments of the poem contain fine things. It would be possible to abstract sentences and paragraphs of the review which would look very good on a dust jacket of the book. But Winters, as in his earlier review of *The Fugitives,* was using *The Bridge* as a means of illustrating the perils of anti-intellectualism. Crane exemplifies, as does the later work of James Joyce, Elizabeth Madox Roberts, and William Carlos Williams, the disintegration of genius in a stylistic automatism, the failure of the understanding to control, order, and fuse perception. Winters was not the same critic who had received the several segments of *The Bridge* between 1926 and 1928. He was no longer appreciative, no longer concerned with felicities rather than with general informing principles that would place all the elements of the poem in an integrated harmonious set of relations. His historical judgment and his moral judgment intervened, so that Crane became exemplary of processes in the history of ideas and of ethics that were deleterious to the total imaginative and intellectual life of poetry. It may seem curious that even in writing the review Winters should have thought of Crane as one of the four or five most important poets of the era,[15] but it was exactly the genius displayed by Crane that led Winters to make him an example; a lesser poet would not bear the burden:

It is possible that Mr. Crane may recover himself. In any event, he has given us, in his first book, several lyrics that one is tempted to call great, and in both books several charming minor lyrics and many magnificent fragments. And one thing he has demonstrated, the impossibility of getting anywhere with the Whitmanian inspiration. No writer of comparable ability has struggled with it before, and, with Mr. Crane's wreckage in view, it seems highly unlikely that any writer of comparable genius will struggle with it again.[16]

In spite of the qualifications and implied defenses of the review that I have made, it is by no means pleasant reading. Its praise is grudging and very qualified; its tone is at times pedantic, at others surly; and the tone overrides any praise. It is no wonder that Crane found it offensive, and with the background of past praise and admiration from Winters, Crane had every reason to be shocked. Several other reviews by friends were at best qualified in their praise, and Allen Tate came very close to Winters's judgment. But Crane already knew of Tate's reservations about *The*

Bridge, and the review was in tone as friendly as its title, "A Distinguished Poet."[17]

Although the correspondence ended with the review, Crane remained at the forefront of Winters's mind for many years. In *Primitivism and Decadence* (1937) Crane is mentioned some twenty-four times; only Williams and Eliot were so frequently cited, and not even Stevens came close to such frequency. Winters wrote two poems on Crane's death, and eventually in 1947 put an end to his long reflections on Crane with "The Significance of *The Bridge* by Hart Crane, or What are We to Think of Professor X?" All this is an epilogue to the correspondence.

VIII

EPILOGUE

Between 1930 and 1934, Crane remained central to Winters's thought and poetic concerns. When his doctoral dissertation was completed (1934) the text was in most respects identical with the ultimate book *Primitivism and Decadence* (1937), and Crane figured largely in his arguments. When he received the news four days after Crane jumped from the poop of the *Orizaba* on April 27, 1932, he was deeply saddened at the death of this very great poet and wrote to Allen Tate with a peculiar blend of loss and self-vindication. He had been reading Crane carefully and had concluded that suicide was the inevitable way out for him, the final result of a century of easily accepted pantheistic mysticism. And the death paralleled Crane's casual acceptance of Harry Crosby's suicide. During the two following years he wrote two poems that pivoted on Crane's death, "The Anniversary, To Achilles Holt," and "Orpheus, In Memory of Hart Crane."[1] The first of these may celebrate an anniversary shared by Holt and Winters; it may refer to the first anniversary of Crane's death, loosely identified with summer. A quart of wine is shared for the parting of two friends; the season momentarily confuses motivation. Earth follows the sun toward its own ultimate dissolution, propelled by forces it cannot control, but in the confusion and the mechanical movement of the earth, man maintains his obligation of free will. Crane's death intervenes and guides the mind to the terrible reminder of human mortality and the possible breakdown of the will:

> Crane is dead at sea. The year
> Dwindles to a purer fear.

"Orpheus, In Memory of Hart Crane" is one of Winters's several classical allegories, and in it he plays rather loosely with the myth. His interest is in the poetic dilemma rather than in decoration. The association of Crane with Orpheus may have come from the presence of Crane's collage of the "Musician Apostolic" in Winters's study, framed and carefully preserved. The poem divides exactly in two, nine lines devoted primarily to the partial resurrection of Eurydice, nine treating the death of Orpheus. In the opening stanza the reference to Zeus's shrine at Dodona is justified only by the legendary antiquity of Orpheus. The line "Wisdom never understood" is cryptic — did the music of Orpheus render wisdom that was not understood or did Orpheus fail to understand a greater wisdom? Or is it impossible for tree, flesh, and stone to comprehend what charms them? Wisdom is at any event a failure, and the song itself seems to be merely illusory, working only while its tones continue. In this version it is not Orpheus's backward glance that reconsigns Eurydice to the underworld but a break in his singing.

> Climbing from the Lethal dead,
> Past the ruined waters' bed,
> In the sleep his music cast
> Tree and flesh and stone were fast —
> As amid Dodona's wood
> Wisdom never understood.
>
> Till the shade his music won
> Shuddered, by a pause undone —
> Silence would not let her stay.

The second section of the poem turns directly to the death of Orpheus, which seems to be willed, a matter of choice rather than victimization. Orpheus gives his flesh in a terrible act. The tongue remains immortal; but the song is unmeaning.

He could go one only way:
By the river, strong with grief,
Gave his flesh beyond belief.

Yet the fingers on the lyre
Spread like an avenging fire.
Crying loud, the immortal tongue,
From the empty body wrung,
Broken in a bloody dream,
Sang unmeaning down the stream.

The poem has admirable things in it, but the collocation of Orpheus with Crane does not seem to add much to either figure—the poem breaks in two. What might serve to unify the two halves of the poem is the sense of the failure, the inutility, of prophecy. There is a kind of glory and a kind of waste. Crane, to Winters's mind, could have been four times the poet he was, great though he was. Taken in those terms, there is a deep sadness in the poem and a relentless judgment. Winters advises that readers of poetry trust the poem rather than the author's ethics, and if one does so, the split in this poem indicates unresolved experience, not fully mastered and comprehended. There is a multiplicity of themes and uncontrolled ambiguity. Does "Wisdom never understood" mean that wisdom never did understand or wisdom never was understood? Is the "as" in the preceding line to be taken as adverb or conjunction? Why is the song "unmeaning" in the closing line? Because of the separation of head from body, the disintegration of perception and meaning? Whose dream is treated in the next to last line? That of Orpheus or that of the Maenads? The split and tension in the poem seem to indicate ambivalence toward the poetic enterprise, and particular trouble when contemplating the work of Crane.

The poem was written while Winters was completing his doctoral dissertation, the core of which is contained in *Primitivism and Decadence*. In that book, Crane is a major figure, and the references to him involve problems of symbolic and structural meaning. Those to Williams, who serves as his counterpart, more frequently concern metrical problems. In this poem Winters faces the emotional rather than theoretical and taxonomic problems raised by the figure of Crane. There is a deeply felt emotional quality to the poem that is, to use a term dear to Winters, untranslatable. The difficulties noted above are not insuperable. There are many better poems by Winters, but this is a remarkable piece of work.

Winters, in the period after Crane's death, could not reject or accept this great and disturbed spirit. He was at the center of the critical and poetic problem, and that problem was at the center of life. Crane was the ultimate outcome of the Romantic tradition in general and the tradition of American transcendentalism in particular. His work was a prime example of "pseudo-reference" because Crane was required to speak of the unknowable in the terms of the knowable. Further, Crane was extremely limited in his possible subject matter; his point of view did not permit exact moral discriminations and made his perception of human experience vague or, in a poem like "Indiana," sentimental and weak. His best work exhibited a fragile relation between the isolated poet and some undetermined reality, identified as Eternity:

> Crane's attitude . . . often suggests a kind of theoretic rejection of all human endeavor in favor of some vaguely apprehended but ecstatically asserted existence of a superior sort. As the exact nature of the superior experience is uncertain, it forms a rather uncertain and infertile source of material for exact poetry; one can write poetry about it only by utilizing in some way more or less metaphorical the realm of experience from which one is trying to escape; but as one *is* endeavoring to escape from this realm, not to master it and understand it, one's feelings about it are certain to be confused, and one's imagery drawn from it is bound to be largely formulary and devoid of meaning. That is, in so far as one endeavors to deal with the Absolute, not as a means of ordering one's moral perception but as the subject itself of perception, one will tend to say nothing, despite the multiplication of words. In *The Dance* there seems to be an effort to apply to each of two mutually exclusive fields the terms of the other. . . .

Crane's best work, such as *Repose of Rivers* and *Voyages II,* is not confused, but one feels that the experience is curiously limited and uncomplicated: it is between the author, isolated from most human complications, and Eternity. Crane becomes in such poems a universal symbol of the human mind in a particular situation, a fact which is the source of his power, but of the human mind in very nearly the simplest form of that situation, a fact which is the source of his limitation.[2]

These poetic powers and limitations were further to be seen as the necessary outgrowth of Crane's Whitmanian point of view. Crane's suicide both troubled and vindicated Winters—troubled him because he liked Crane and admired much of his work; vindicated him because so far as Winters was concerned a world without some moral base for discrimination of value was not humanly habitable. As early as 1929 he had suggested to Eugene Jolas that his surrender to the unconscious left him with only two alternatives, the abandonment of that surrender or "the suicide of a gentleman."[3] Jeffers's sense of the meaninglessness of human life, taken literally, would also lead to suicide.[4] Crane, unlike Jolas and Jeffers, had taken his position to its ultimate necessary conclusion:

It may seem a hard thing to say of that troubled and magnificent spirit, Hart Crane, that we shall remember him chiefly for his having shown us a new mode of damnation, yet it is for this that we remember Orestes, and Crane has in addition the glory of being, if not his own Aeschylus, perhaps, in some fragmentary manner, his own Euripides.[5]

Crane was a tragic figure and his own tragedian.

After the publication of *Primitivism and Decadence,* Crane held a less prominent place in Winters's criticism and was very infrequently mentioned. When he collected his three critical books under the title *In Defense of Reason,* however, Crane reappeared, and in the concluding essay became Winters's chief example of the dangers and follies of the tradition flowing from Emerson through Whitman. The essay "The Significance of *The Bridge* by

Hart Crane, or What Are We to Think of Professor X?" summa-
rizes and extends the point of view already developed in less systematic form in Winters's earlier work. The essay is well known and
is sometimes adduced as final proof of Winters's wrong-headed-
ness and heartlessness. To anyone who has followed the present
text, the essay should come as no surprise. In it Winters decries
Emerson for placing impulse above reason and constructing an
optique that makes the discrimination of values impossible. Whitman comes under the same condemnation and Crane is given as
the disastrous end product of mystical pantheism. Professor X
represents those genteel scholars who simply do not take thought
or literature seriously. Crane is the serious poet who lives out in
his work, life, and death the ideas that are at the heart of American transcendentalism and of the Romantic movement generally.

The essay is extremely personal, and in it Winters makes use of
his correspondence with Crane and talks in moving terms of his
four evenings of conversation with Crane. Primarily, however, he
is concerned with Crane as example rather than friend, and it
should be remembered that Crane and Winters were never genuinely close friends in the sense that Tate and Crane were, or
Waldo Frank and Crane or Malcolm Cowley and Crane. Winters
never had to put up with the drunkenness, the furniture smash-
ing, or the telephoned apologies at four o'clock in the morning.
He knew neither the full rewards nor the vicissitudes of friendship
with Crane which such people as Tate, Cowley, and Josephson
knew only too well. There were for Winters no softening forces
such as arise from shared pleasures and exasperated forgiveness;
Crane could remain a literary type without the full features of a
complex remembered human figure. Nothing like Malcolm Cowley's reminiscences clouded the generalized idea with affectionate
trivia:

> Hart, Hart. . . . He did so much that was outrageous, but
> so much that was unaffectedly kind or exuberant and so
> much that kept us entertained. Nobody yawned when Hart
> was there. He liked to dance — aggressively, acrobatically,
> without much knowledge of steps, but with an unerring sense

of rhythm; he swept his partner off her feet and usually she followed him with a look of delicious terror. He liked to do solo dances too, including one that he called the Gazotsky because it was vaguely Russian. He liked anything sung by Sophie Tucker or Marlene Dietrich and burst into admiring chuckles as he listened. He liked to hear nonsense poems, the bawdier the better, and he wrote a few of them. I remember one about Sappho that he used to recite:

> Said the poetess Sappho of Greece,
> "Ah, better by far than a piece
>   Is to have my pudenda
>   Rubbed hard by the enda
> The little pink nose of my niece."

Somebody repeated Hart's lines to Norman Douglas, in a slightly altered version, and he promptly included them in his famous anthology of dirty limericks. I forget what Hart said when he saw the book.

There is so much I forget about him, as if part of my own life had been erased, and so much I remember too.[6]

This was not a problem for Winters. He and Cowley could agree that the poems written to complete *The Bridge* in 1929 weakened the effect of the whole, that Crane's talent deteriorated irreparably after he completed "The River" in 1928, and above all they could agree about Crane's poetic devotion:

> Writing poetry—not poems written, but those to come—was the motive and justification for all his vices, for life itself. He would never be an old man using his picturesque decay as an excuse for getting drinks on the house. With no more poems he could be confident of writing, now that his method had betrayed him, he had no reason for being.[7]

Cowley sees Crane through the scrim of memory, Winters sees him more abstractly, but their ultimate conclusions are not terribly different. Cowley's beautiful memoir of Crane is, like the other portraits in *A Second Flowering*, informed with Cowley's special humanism and the fond generosity of his memory. Winters's essay is polemical in intent, written from exasperation not with Crane but with Professor X, who had never read a book that he would be willing to quarrel over, to whom literature was a mere amenity. Winters would certainly be willing to quarrel over a book and over a system of thought that he considered pernicious.

> The doctrine of Emerson and Whitman, if really put into practice, should naturally lead to suicide: in the first place, if the impulses are indulged systematically and passionately, they can lead only to madness; in the second place, death, according to the doctrine, is not only a release from suffering but is also and inevitably the way to beatitude. There is no question, according to the doctrine, of moral preparation for salvation; death leads automatically to salvation. During the last year and a half of Crane's life, to judge from the accounts of those who were with him in Mexico, he must have been insane or drunk or both almost without interruption; but before this time he must have contemplated the possibilities of suicide. When his friend Harry Crosby leapt from a high window in one of the eastern cities, I wrote Crane a note of condolence and asked him to express my sympathy to Mrs. Crosby. Crane replied somewhat casually that I need not feel disturbed about the affair, that he was fairly sure Crosby had regarded it as a great adventure.[8]

Crane's letter of January 27, 1930 (pp. 141-142 above) shows that Winters or his memory was bending the truth a little, and Winters had no way to know that Crosby had chosen a much more elaborate manner of suicide than simple defenestration.[9] Nor could he have known that Crane's brevity was a way of avoiding an agony that obsessed him for months. What mattered to Winters was the moral scheme and issue — Crane's philosophical commitment made suicide a reasonable and even inevitable outcome of his life.

> The Emersonian doctrine, which is merely the romantic doctrine with a New England emotional coloration, should naturally result in madness if one really lived it; it should

result in literary confusion if one really wrote it. Crane accepted it; he lived it; he wrote it.... [10]

This statement is followed by a paragraph that I have already quoted (chap. 6, p. 109), but at the close of this study it deserves to be repeated:

> Professor X says, or since he is a gentleman and a scholar, he implies, that Crane was merely a fool, that he ought to have known better. But the fact of the matter is, that Crane was not a fool. I knew Crane, as I know Professor X, and I am reasonably certain that Crane was incomparably the more intelligent man. As to Crane's ideas, they were merely those of Professor X, neither better nor worse; and for the rest, he was able to write great poetry. In spite of popular and even academic prejudices to the contrary, it takes a very highly developed intelligence to write great poetry, even a little of it. So far as I am concerned, I would gladly emulate Odysseus, if I could, and go down to the shadows for another hour's conversation with Crane on the subject of poetry; whereas, politeness permitting, I seldom go out of my way to discuss poetry with Professor X. [11]

In what would be Winters's last and presumably definitive comment on his sense of Crane as man and poet, there is an underlying respect and affection. If he had known Crane better, he could not have written the essay; he knew Crane barely well enough to use him as an exemplary figure, a kind of form in the history of the human imagination and conscience:

> Crane...had the absolute seriousness which goes with genius and sanctity; one might describe him as a saint of the wrong religion. He had not the critical intelligence to see what was wrong with his doctrine, but he had the courage of his convictions, the virtue of integrity, and he deserves our respect. He has the value of a thoroughgoing demonstration. He embodies perfectly the concepts which for nearly a century have been generating some of the most cherished principles of our literature, our education, our politics, and our personal morals. If Crane is too strong a dose for us, and we

must yet retain the principles which he represents, we may still, of course, look to Professor X as a model. But we shall scarcely get anything better unless we change our principles.[12]

Two decades had by now passed since Crane wrote first to Winters and asserted their common ground in the work of Whitman. Whether Winters objected at the time we do not know; by 1947 the Whitman tradition was anathema to Winters, and he saw in it the cause of Crane's deterioration and death. From this point on, Winters hardly refers to Crane. In his last critical work, *Forms of Discovery,* Crane is mentioned only twice; none of Crane's poems is included in his final anthology, *Quest for Reality.* There was nothing more to say. For twenty years Crane was central to Winters's poetics, and this essay is Winters's final farewell; it is close to being a rite of exorcism.

APPENDIX

William Dinsmore Briggs was Winters's mentor during his years as a graduate student at Stanford and his protector during his early years as a member of the English department. Briggs's associations with Stanford were long and deep. He was graduated from Stanford in 1896, went on to graduate study at Johns Hopkins and finally at Harvard, where he took his doctorate in 1900. He then taught in the eastern United States and returned to Stanford in 1906; he was chairman of the English department from 1926 until his death in 1941.

Briggs had the reputation of being a great teacher who did not publish. He did publish one book, an edition of Marlowe's *Edward II* with a lengthy introduction. He also published articles and notes on Ben Jonson and other matters having to do with the Renaissance until 1923. The Stanford Archives do not record any publications after that date. Two events may explain his abandoning scholarship in favor of teaching and administration. In 1924 his son and only child died, which may partly account for his paternal devotion to his students and younger colleagues. That shock was great, but another occurred at approximately the same time. Briggs had been preparing a definitive edition of Ben Jonson; the first volume of the great Herford-Simpson edition appeared in 1925, so that his lifework as a scholar lost its meaning.

For whatever reason, he put his main energies into his teaching. His courses in the Renaissance, especially in the lyric poetry, were evidently models and account for Winters's absorption in Jonson, Gascoigne, Googe, and Herrick. Winters was not his sole admirer. J. V. Cunningham kept notes on his lectures so full as to be practically verbatim. Briggs encouraged his students to read as widely as possible in philosophy. Virgil Whitaker regrets that he did not follow his advice—but Winters did. Philosophically, Briggs was a skeptic with a strong sense of order, a description that equally fits Winters. It was Briggs who encouraged Winters to study American literature, thus accounting for the switch from modern—what was then "contemporary"—poetry to the studies in *Maule's Curse* and *The Anatomy of Nonsense* of the biases and continuities of American thought and art of the nineteenth century.

Winters wrote three poems that refer to Briggs: "To William Dinsmore Briggs Conducting his Seminar," "For the Opening of the William Dinsmore Briggs Room," and "Dedication for a Book of Criticism, To *W. D. Briggs.*" The last of these poems indicates Winters's sense of personal debt, especially in the closing stanza:

> In the motions of your thought
> I a plan and model sought;
> My deficiencies but gauge
> My own talents and the age;
> What is good from you I took:
> Then, in justice, take my book.

But it was not only as teacher that Briggs had a beneficent effect on Winters. To those who remember the American academy before World War II, it should be surprising that Winters was kept on the Stanford staff. His dissertation was on contemporary poetry; he wrote and published his own poetry; his other chief field of interest was American literature. None of these subjects and activities was widely honored in the American academy of that time. Moreover, Winters was primarily a practical critic and moralist and, unlike most academic figures of the time, was neither historian nor biographer but used scholarly knowledge for primarily evaluative purposes.

When Briggs died, he was succeeded as chairman by A. G. Kennedy, who called Winters into his office and informed him that his publications were a disgrace to the department. Kennedy was an Anglo-Saxon scholar and a bibliographer, and his dislike of Winters was heartily reciprocated. Winters was so disturbed that he attempted to enlist in the Army, thinking that his linguistic skills would be useful in Army Intelligence. His age and health were against him. He then tried to move to several small colleges in California, and when those efforts were fruitless, in 1944 he prepared a twelve-page mimeographed *vita* which he sent to various English departments throughout the country to accompany an application for a position as teacher of English. At the time Winters was an associate professor with tenure but no likelihood of promotion and an annual salary of $3,500.

When Kennedy was succeeded by Richard Foster Jones, Jones took an active interest in Winters's well-being, as did Jones's successor Virgil Whitaker, so that he was promoted and received annual wage increases. Even so, he was not — for a man of his distinction — at all well paid. In 1953 as an associate professor at Berkeley, I was receiving the same salary that Winters received as a full professor at Stanford. I was thirty-three years old; Winters was fifty-three. Salaries at Stanford were notoriously low during that period, but Winters was, to the world outside, the most important member of the department. I do not bring these matters up to embarrass Stanford, which has gone well past those days, has a fine department of English and great flexibility and receptivity to fresh ideas, but to explain Winters's debt to Briggs and give some of the background of his academic career. His status at Stanford steadily improved over the years, and when he was appointed Albert Guerard Professor of English in 1962, he was quite well paid.

I also think that Winters's career might restore some perspective on what the New Criticism — which now seems like the Old Orthodoxy — was in the early days of Winters, Burke, Tate, Ransom, and Blackmur. It was not academically respectable, as Kennedy's reaction to Winters suggests. It was practical, it was moral, and it was experimental. University faculties and administrations, with very few exceptions, looked on it as having at best dubious merit. Of the American New Critics, only Winters and Ransom held academic posts before World War II, and Winters's difficulties at Stanford during Kennedy's chairmanship parallel Ransom's difficulties at Vanderbilt. It is really high time for a proper examination, in historical perspective, of the criticism conducted in this country in the period before the outbreak of World War II. As Robert Lowell remarked in his *Paris Review* interview, during that period young writers found the excitement in new articles by Tate, Blackmur, Burke, Winters, and Ransom, which is normally reserved for the appearance of a fine new poem or work of fiction. In those days, criticism was a new and exciting form of art, as Winters's criticism, at its best, always was. It is to his everlasting credit that Briggs had the great good sense, as Jones and Whitaker did after him, to see the value in Winters's poetry and criticism, that is, the value of art.

NOTES

Preface

1. *The Letters of Hart Crane,* ed. Brom Weber (Berkeley and Los Angeles, 1965), p. 278.

2. Ibid., p. 284.

3. Ibid., p. 288.

4. See *The Uncollected Essays and Reviews of Yvor Winters,* ed. Francis Murphy (Chicago, 1973), pp. 47-50, 73-82, 100-111. Yvor Winters, *In Defense of Reason* (New York, 1947), pp. 577-603. No poems are included in Winters's last book, an anthology selected by Winters and completed by Kenneth Fields, *Quest for Reality* (Chicago, 1969).

5. Yvor Winters, *The Early Poems of Yvor Winters, 1920-28* (Chicago, 1966).

6. Janet Lewis Winters kindly gave me this information and other data in a series of interviews.

7. Robert Lowell, *Poetry* (April 1961), pp. 40-41.

Chapter I: A Meeting of Minds

1. Yvor Winters, *Forms of Discovery* (Chicago, 1967), pp. 328-329. The description occurs in his discussion of Adelaide Crapsey.

2. *The Early Poems of Yvor Winters, 1920-28* (Chicago, 1966). The "Introduction" (pp. 7-16) contains biographical material.

3. Winters's letters to Tate have been used with the permission of Janet Lewis Winters and the Princeton University Library, where the letters are deposited with the papers of Allen Tate. Cassettes of the interviews with Janet Lewis are currently in the Bancroft Library of the University of California at Berkeley.

4. Cowley is talking about Crane's intense labor on *Blue Juniata*. The entire comment on Crane's activity should be consulted. Susan Jenkins Brown, *Robber Rocks: Letters and Memories of Hart Crane* (Middletown, Conn., 1969), p. 106.

5. *Poetry* (October 1926), p. 41. The University of Chicago has Winters's original letter in its Joseph Regenstein Library.

6. Hart Crane, *Complete Poems and Selected Letters and Prose,* ed. Brom Weber (New York, 1966), pp. 23-24. Crane's anger was not entirely justified. Marianne Moore wrote him a very courteous letter requesting permission to make certain changes, and Crane's reply accepted the changes: "I agree with you that the enclosed version of THE WINE MENAGERIE contains the essential elements of the original poem, and inasmuch as I admire the sensibility and skill of your rearrangement of the poem I should be glad to have it so printed in The Dial. The title, "Again," of course will supplant the original one." The letter is signed "Gratefully yours, Hart Crane." Crane's gratitude may have been largely financial, but with this letter in mind, Miss Moore had every right to be annoyed by Crane's expressed annoyance with her editing. The letter is in the Beinecke Library at Yale University.

7. Basil Lubbock, *The China Clippers* (Glasgow, 1914). Although the book is not indexed, I have searched it thoroughly. Crane did not have at hand Lubbock's *The Log of the Cutty Sark* (Glasgow, 1914) while composing "Cutty Sark," though he may have seen it later. His friend William Slater Brown owned a copy. So far as I can tell, *Nimbus* does not appear in either book, though Crane may have found the name elsewhere. My suspicion is that he invented it, in spite of his claim that all the ships named in the poem had actually existed.

8. Yvor Winters, *Uncollected Essays and Reviews* (Chicago, 1973), p. 80. Reprinted from *Poetry Magazine* for June 1930.

9. The word is "persistent" in printed versions of Winters's poem "Nocturne."

Chapter II: *White Buildings*

1. William Carlos Williams, *Imaginations* (New York, 1970), p. 15.

2. For the best access to the history of the early publication of *White Buildings,* see Joseph Schwartz and Robert C. Schweik, *Hart Crane: A Descriptive Bibliography* (Pittsburgh, 1972), pp. 3-10. *White Buildings* has recently been republished with the original foreword by Allen Tate and a new introduction by John Logan (New York, 1972).

3. *The Letters of Hart Crane,* ed. Brom Weber (Berkeley and Los Angeles, 1965), p. 282.

4. Ibid., p. 281.

5. Schwartz and Schweik, *Hart Crane*, p. 7. See also Logan (n. 2 above).

6. Leonard Greenbaum, *The Hound & Horn, The History of a Literary Quarterly*. Studies in American Literature (The Hague, 1966), VI, 177.

7. *Letters*, p. 284.

8. Winters's review of *White Buildings* with Harriet Monroe's note was published in *Poetry* (April 1927), pp. 47-51. It has been reprinted (without Monroe's note) in *Yvor Winters: Uncollected Essays and Reviews*, ed. Francis Murphy (Chicago, 1973), pp. 47-50. Tate's Foreword has been reprinted in the Logan edition of *White Buildings* and in Tate's *Memoirs and Opinions, 1926-74* (Chicago, 1975), pp. 110-114.

Chapter III: Emerging Differences

For discussion of Winters's early poetry see Grosvenor E. Powell, "Mythical and Smoky Soil: Imagism and the Aboriginal in the Early Poetry of Yvor Winters," *Southern Review* (Spring 1975). For a general discussion of the poetry, see Howard Kaye, "The Post-Symbolist Poetry of Yvor Winters," *Southern Review* (Winter 1971), pp. 176-197.

1. Published by Alan Swallow, available through The Swallow Press, Chicago.

2. Yvor Winters, *The Early Poems of Yvor Winters, 1920-28* (Chicago, 1966), p. 49.

3. "The Muses Out of Work," *The New Republic* (May 11, 1927), pp. 319-321. Reprinted with additional material in *The Shores of Light* (New York, 1952), pp. 197-211.

4. Yvor Winters, *The Uncollected Essays and Reviews of Yvor Winters*, ed. Francis Murphy (Chicago, 1973), pp. 194-215.

5. Yvor Winters, *Early Poems*, p. 86.

6. Ibid., p. 85.

7. Ibid., p. 98. Also in Winters, *Collected Poems* (Denver, 1960), p. 33. Like all Alan Swallow books, this text is available now through The Swallow Press, Chicago.

8. Yvor Winters, "By Way of Clarification," *Twentieth Century Literature* (October 1964), p. 131.

9. Kenneth Fields, "The Free Verse of Yvor Winters and William Carlos Williams," *Southern Review* (Summer 1967), pp. 710-711.

10. Jacques Loeb, *The Mechanistic Conception of Life* (Chicago, 1912). For Loeb's theory of the chrystal see his *The Organism as a Whole, from a Physiochemical Viewpoint* (New York and London,

1916), especially "The Specific Difference Between Living and Dead Matter and the Question of the Origin of Life," pp. 14-39.

11. W. A. Swanberg, *Dreiser* (New York, 1965), p. 236.

12. "By Way of Clarification" (see n. 8), p. 132.

13. Ibid., p. 131.

14. This letter is now in the hands of Janet Lewis Winters and is reproduced with the permission of Mr. Tate.

15. Crane's letter appears in *The Letters of Hart Crane,* ed. Brom Weber, p. 288.

Chapter IV: Progress on *The Bridge*

1. Joseph Schwartz and Robert C. Schweik, *Hart Crane: A Descriptive Bibliography* (Pittsburg, 1972), p. 16.

2. *The Letters of Hart Crane,* ed. Brom Weber (Berkeley and Los Angeles, 1965), p. 272.

3. John Unterecker, *Voyager: A Life of Hart Crane* (New York, 1969), pp. 477-478.

4. Anonymous, "Briefer Mention," *The Dial* (May 1927), p. 432.

5. Quoted in Unterecker, *Voyager,* p. 495.

Chapter V: A Threatening Letter

1. Edmund Wilson, "The Muses Out of Work," *The New Republic* (May 11, 1927), pp. 319-321. Reprinted with additional material in *The Shores of Light* (New York, 1952), pp. 197-211.

2. Ibid., p. 200.

3. Ibid., p. 201.

4. Ibid.

Chapter VI: Their Only Meeting

1. Malcolm Cowley, *A Second Flowering: Works and Days of the Lost Generation* (New York, 1973), p. 210.

2. Yvor Winters, *Early Poems, 1920-28* (Chicago, 1966), p. 13.

3. John Unterecker, *Voyager: A Life of Hart Crane* (New York, 1969), p. 574.

4. Yvor Winters, *In Defense of Reason* (New York, 1947), pp. 599-600.

5. From "On a View of Pasadena from the Hills," *Collected Poems,* p. 64.

6. Winters, *In Defense of Reason,* pp. 589-590.

7. See "The Realization," *Collected Poems,* p. 46, lines 10-11.

8. *Poetry* (April 1928), pp. 46-47.

9. *The New Republic* (March 21, 1928), p. 165.

10. "Mr. Moon's Notebook," *The Saturday Review of Literature* (March 10, 1928), p. 665. Winters's reply was not printed.

11. "Fugitives," *The Uncollected Essays and Reviews of Yvor Winters* (Chicago, 1973), p. 55. Originally in *Poetry* (February 1928), pp. 102-107.

Chapter VII: The Last Phase

1. *The Letters of Hart Crane,* ed. Brom Weber (Berkeley and Los Angeles, 1965), pp. 347-348.

2. Yvor Winters, *The Uncollected Essays and Reviews,* ed. Francis Murphy (Chicago, 1973), pp. 255-270.

3. Yvor Winters, *In Defense of Reason* (New York, 1947), p. 601. See also Grosvenor E. Powell, "Mythical and Smoky Soil: Imagism and the Aboriginal in the Early Poetry of Yvor Winters," *The Southern Review* (Spring 1975), see especially pp. 310-315.

4. Winters, *The Uncollected Essays and Reviews,* pp. 226-227.

5. Ibid., pp. 227-228.

6. Ibid., p. 266.

7. Ibid., p. 247.

8. Ibid., p. 216.

9. Ibid., p. 222.

10. *The Letters of Hart Crane,* p. 352.

11. Winters, *The Uncollected Essays and Reviews,* pp. 216-217.

12. Ibid., p. 76.

13. Ibid., p. 77.

14. Ibid.

15. Yvor Winters, "Poetry, Morality and Criticism," *The Critique of Humanism,* ed. C. Hartley Grattan (New York, 1930), p. 316.

16. *The Uncollected Essays and Reviews,* p. 82.

17. *The Hound and Horn* (July-Summer 1930), pp. 580-585.

Chapter VIII: Epilogue

1. Yvor Winters, *Collected Poems* (Denver, 1960), pp. 81, 85.

2. Yvor Winters, *In Defense of Reason* (New York, 1947), pp. 27-28.

3. Yvor Winters, *Uncollected Essays and Reviews,* ed. Francis Murphy (Chicago, 1973), p. 250.

4. Winters, *In Defense of Reason,* p. 32.

5. Ibid., p. 101.

6. Malcolm Cowley, *A Second Flowering: Works and Days of the Lost Generation* (New York, 1973), pp. 204-205.

7. Ibid., p. 211.

8. Winters, *In Defense of Reason,* p. 590.

9. John Unterecker, *Voyager: A Life of Hart Crane* (New York, 1969), p. 610.

10. Winters, *In Defense of Reason,* p. 599.

11. Ibid., pp. 599-600.

12. Ibid., pp. 602-603.

BIBLIOGRAPHY

Brown, Susan Jenkins. *Robber Rocks: Letters and Memories of Hart Crane, 1923-1932*. Middletown: Wesleyan University Press, 1969.

Butterfield, R. W. *The Broken Arc: A Study of Hart Crane*. Edinburgh: Oliver and Boyd, 1969.

Cowley, Malcolm. *A Second Flowering: Works and Days of the Lost Generation*. New York: The Viking Press, 1973.

Crane, Hart. *The Letters of Hart Crane, 1916-1932*. Ed. Brom Weber. Berkeley and Los Angeles: University of California Press, 1965.

——— . *The Complete Poems and Selected Letters and Prose*. Ed. Brom Weber. Garden City, N. Y.: Doubleday (Anchor Books), 1966.

——— . *The Bridge*. Facsimile Edition. Commentaries by Waldo Frank and Thomas A. Vogler. New York: Liveright, 1970.

——— . *White Buildings*. Facsimile Edition. Reproduces Allen Tate's Foreword as "Introduction," and includes a new "Foreword" by John Logan. New York: Liveright, 1972.

——— . *Letters of Hart Crane and His Family*. Ed. Thomas S. W. Lewis. New York: Columbia University Press, 1974.

Fields, Kenneth. "The Free Verse of Yvor Winters and William Carlos Williams." *Southern Review,* Summer 1967, pp. 764-775.

Greenbaum, Leonard. "The Hound and Horn: The History of a Literary Quarterly." *Studies in American Literature*. Vol. VI. The Hague: 1966.

Kaye, Howard. "The Post-Symbolist Poetry of Yvor Winters." *Southern Review,* Winter 1971, pp. 176-197.

Lewis, R. W. B. *The Poetry of Hart Crane: A Critical Study*. Princeton: Princeton University Press, 1967.

Loeb, Jacques. *The Mechanistic Conception of Life*. Chicago: University of Chicago Press, 1912.

Lohf, Kenneth A., and Eugene P. Sheehy. *Yvor Winters: A Bibliography*. Denver: Alan Swallow, 1959.
———. *The Literary Manuscripts of Hart Crane*. Columbus: Ohio State University Press, 1967.
Paul, Sherman. *Hart's Bridge*. Urbana: University of Illinois Press, 1972.
Powell, Grosvenor E. "Mythical and Smoky Soil: Imagism and the Aboriginal in the Early Poetry of Yvor Winters." *Southern Review*, Spring 1975, pp. 300-317.
Schwartz, Joseph. *Hart Crane: An Annotated Critical Bibliography*. New York: David Lewis, 1970.
Schwartz, Joseph, and Robert C. Schweik. *Hart Crane: A Descriptive Bibliography*. Pittsburgh: University of Pittsburgh Press, 1972.
Tate, Allen. *Essays of Four Decades*. Chicago: The Swallow Press, 1968.
———. *Memoirs and Opinions*. Chicago: The Swallow Press, 1975.
Unterecker, John. *Voyager: A Life of Hart Crane*. New York: Farrar, Straus, Giroux, 1969.
Uroff, M. D. *Hart Crane: The Patterns of His Poetry*. Urbana: University of Illinois Press, 1974.
Weber, Brom. *Hart Crane: A Biographical and Critical Study*. New York: The Bodley Press, 1948.
Wilson, Edmund. "The Muses Out of Work." *The Shores of Light*. New York: Farrar, Straus and Young, 1952. Pp. 197-211.
Winters, Yvor. "Poetry, Morality and Criticism." *The Critique of Humanism*. Ed. C. Hartley Grattan. New York: Brewer and Warren, 1930. Pp. 301-333.
———. *In Defense of Reason*. New York: The Swallow Press and William Morrow and Co., 1947.
———. *The Function of Criticism: Problems and Exercises*. Denver: Alan Swallow, 1957.
———. *Collected Poems*. Denver: Alan Swallow, 1960.
———. "By Way of Clarification." *Twentieth Century Literature*, October 1964, pp. 130-135.
———. *The Early Poems of Yvor Winters, 1920-28*. Denver: Alan Swallow, 1966.
———. *Forms of Discovery*. Denver: Alan Swallow, 1967.
———. *The Uncollected Essays and Reviews*. Ed. Francis Murphy. Chicago: The Swallow Press, 1973.
Winters, Yvor, and Kenneth Fields. *Quest for Reality*. Chicago: The Swallow Press, 1969.

INDEX

The Index was prepared by me with the help of Penelope Nesbitt. I have listed names and titles and have made no attempt to provide a subject index. The recurrence of Allen Tate's name was so frequent that I thought at one time of simply saying Tate, Allen, passim. But he and Winters and Crane will in the history of our poetry be seen as an inseparable trio, so that it is important to note the frequency of his appearance in the text. The number of entries is very large for so relatively short a book, but Crane and Winters ranged over a large body of literature and a large gallery of literary figures of past and present, and that is one of the interests in the relations between Crane and Winters. They were immensely curious and energetic men with an extraordinary range of interests. I have not indexed the notes and bibliography.